Battl

1066

The battles of York, Stamford Bridge and Hastings

With the continued expansion of the Battleground series a **Battleground Series Club** has been formed to benefit the reader. The purpose of the Club is to keep members informed of new titles and to offer many other reader-benefits. Membership is free and by registering an interest you can help us predict print runs and thus assist us in maintaining the quality and prices at their present levels.

Please call the office 01226 734555, or send your name and address along with a request for more information to:

Battleground Series Club Pen & Sword Books Ltd,
47 Church Street, Barnsley, South Yorkshire S70 2AS

Battleground Britain

1066
The battles of York, Stamford Bridge and Hastings

Peter Marren

Thoughts must be the braver, hearts the more valiant,
courage the greater, as our strength grows less.
Anon - The Battle of Maldon

A strange kind of battle, one side attacking with all mobility,
the other withstanding, as though rooted to the soil.
William of Poitiers - Gesta Guillelmi

Pen & Sword
MILITARY

To my Godson William Finnie
in the confidence he will grow up more
like King Harold than King William

First published in Great Britain in 2004 by
Leo Cooper

Reprinted in this format in 2010 by
Pen and Sword Military
An imprint of
Pen & Sword Books Ltd
47 Church Street
Barnsley
South Yorkshire
S70 2AS

ISBN 978 85052 953 1

A CIP catalogue record for this book is
available from the British Library

Printed and bound in England
By CPI

Pen & Sword Books Ltd incorporates the Imprints of Pen & Sword Aviation,
Pen & Sword Family History, Pen & Sword Maritime, Pen & Sword Military,
Wharncliffe Local History,
Pen & Sword Select, Pen & Sword Military Classics, Leo Cooper, Remember When,
Seaforth Publishing and Frontline Publishing

For a complete list of Pen & Sword titles please contact
PEN & SWORD BOOKS LIMITED
47 Church Street, Barnsley, South Yorkshire, S70 2AS, England
E-mail: enquiries@pen-and-sword.co.uk
Website: www.pen-and-sword.co.uk

CONTENTS

INTRODUCTION

1066 is, famously, the best known date in history. As Sellar and Yeatman, the authors of *1066 and All That*, remind us, it was the year William conquered England 'at the Battle of Senlac (Ten Sixty-six)'. In their view, the Conquest 'was a Good Thing, as from this time onwards England stopped being conquered and thus was able to become Top Nation'. In the same spirit, drivers passing Pevensey or Rye will see a brown 'heritage' sign welcoming them to '1066 Country'. To English travellers, at least, no further explanation is necessary. This is where 1066 happened. Perhaps the picture most people see when they think of 1066 is King Harold with an arrow sticking out of one eye. When the proposed bypass at Hastings was in the news a few years ago, a cartoon appeared in a national newspaper showing two men standing over the stricken king, one of whom is saying: 'if only we'd had a bypass none of this would have happened'. Rather funnier is the one about Harold's 'famous last words': "I spy with my little eye, something beginning with 'A'.....". The same universal familiarity with 1066 is assumed by the builder in Rye, who trades under the name of William the Concreter. Everyone understands the joke.

All the same, one wonders what people expect to see in '1066 Country'. There are not many physical reminders of 1066. The coastline has changed since then: the site of the Norman landing is dry land and the Saxon port of Hastings lies under the waves. The windy ridge where Harold had his rendezvous with the arrow was levelled and built over shortly after the battle. Indeed one has to work hard to find one stone on top of another that was there in 1066: the Roman shell of Pevensey Castle, perhaps the motte at Hastings Castle, a few church towers, like that of St Mary in the Marsh, then built on an island, like a lighthouse, surrounded by tidal marshes, now in a yellow sea of oil-seed rape. But there is scarcely a surviving house, wall, tree or mound that Duke William might have noticed on his way to the battle, or that Harold would have known when he visited his manors at Crowhurst or Whatlington.

On the other hand, one can tread with confidence in the footsteps of the men of 1066, both in the south, at Pevensey, Hastings and, above all, at Battle, and in the north, at York, Riccall and Stamford Bridge. The battlefield of Hastings is in the care of English Heritage and visitors can choose between a variety of interpretative media, from ambulatory headphones to a film in which three (real) characters from 1066 tell their stories, the Englishman in accents rustic, the Norman in a snooty drawl ('Such sport of war we had this day'). Much

The battlefield at Hastings: parkland, a ruined abbey and some ponds.

of the battlefield is open to the public, and is rewarding to explore. At the nearest weekend to the anniversary of the battle there is a re-enactment by the Viking Society, involving authentic-looking hauberks, helmets, axes and bows. A quarter of a million people visit the battlefield of Hastings each year; more than ten times as many as took part in the battle! In the north it is different. Few people visit Fulford or Stamford Bridge, where the modern bridge is in the 'wrong' place, and the most vivid reminder of the battle is the pub-sign of a Viking 'berserker'. But, unlike Hastings, mass graves have been discovered at Fulford and Riccall, and at York there is a sensational museum of life during the Viking period at Coppergate. There is an interesting even-handedness about the battles of 1066: the English, Normans and Vikings each won a battle. Perhaps the Normans won the race because they did not have to fight a second battle. King Harold and his Viking name sake, Harald Hardrada, both did, and both of them lost it.

1066 is perhaps the first time in English history when one can get to know the main characters a little, and discover something about the motives behind their actions, and their political background. The story used to be taught at schools, with the aid of the Bayeux Tapestry, and Hastings was one of our set-piece battles, along with Crècy, Agincourt, Naseby and Blenheim. We learned about the shield-wall, of the feigned retreats, and how William directed his archers to fire high, thus fatally wounding Harold in the eye.Though we were nearly all on Harold's side, we were taught that the battle was probably a good thing in the end, since it was the start of real history, with castles, cathedrals and memorable kings and queens.The period before 1066 tended to a bit of a blur, when, apart from King Arthur and King Alfred, no one was memorable, and nothing much happened apart from the Vikings and the Lindisfarne Gospels.

In terms of children's history, then, 1066 stood at the crossroads between the unknown and the more familiar, between prehistory and history. In at least one sense this divide is real. The Battle of Hastings created historians, men like Orderic Vitalis or William of Malmesbury, who not only considered that events were worth recording, but attempted to make sense of them. It is as if the 'exciting times' of 1066 made people start thinking about their past. They wrote about 1066 in what, compared with earlier periods, seems like minute scrutiny. But that is not to say that a battle fought nearly a thousand years ago can be reconstructed in the same way as Waterloo or the Zulu War. The stories about Hastings, and, to a degree, also Fulford and Stamford Bridge, are contradictory.They come down to us filtered through the minds of Norman and English clerical writers of the eleventh and twelfth century who did not interpret events in the way a modern military historian would. To try to understand what happened, and why, we need to make an adjustment from our world to theirs. The language of the eleventh century was more suited to rhetoric and tale-telling than sober reporting. The scribes had no exact way of describing military ordnance, or the appearance of battlefields, or of the military manoeuvres that took place, not least because none of them had ever experienced anything like Hastings or Stamford Bridge. When stumbling for the right word, they used metaphor or turned to the classics for models.But even so, for Hastings at least, there are what sound like eyewitness testimonies, old soldier's tales, that bring you back to earth with a bump.When they do, it is as if the still figures of the Bayeux Tapestry have come to life.

There have been many accounts of 1066 and the Battle of Hastings, long and short, popular and scholarly. In my own contribution to the pile, I have tried to pay proper respect to the sources, and have, as far as possible, allowed the voices of the eleventh century to speak. There is speculation and analysis in these pages, but not, I hope, invention. No writer of 1066 and all that needs to 'sex up' his report; the drama of 1066 needs no fiction. I have deliberately not presented these events as though they happened recently. We see the age only at a great distance, through distorting glass, and its people were not like us; their world was different to ours in ways we can scarely imagine. All the same, human qualities are constant enough for us to gain at least an impression of what William the Conqueror was like and why Harold deserved a better fate. It might be as well to say at the outset that I am sorry the Normans won!Alone of all the great men of that year, Harold appears genuinely likeable, and seems to have been motivated by patriotism as much as by personal ambition.Had he won the Battle of Hastings, he would have been acclaimed as a saviour of his country to compare with Nelson or Churchill. As it is, he is the fall guy with an arrow in his eye, without a single statue or stone to mark his memory.In death as in life he had no luck.

One other matter to bear in mind is that the events of 1066 are dated according to the old calendar which one needs to 'seasonally adjust' by adding eleven days. Hence the Battle of Hastings, fought on 14 October 1066, was 'our' 25 October, when leaves were falling and dusk arrived between five and six. Stamford Bridge, on 25 September, was our 6 October, and probably one of the last warm days that year.

TIMETABLE OF THE MAIN EVENTS OF 1066

5 January: Edward the Confessor dies at Westminster. Harold is crowned the next day.

24 April: Halley's comet appears in the sky.

Early May: Tostig raids the Isle of Wight and the Sussex coast.

Late May: Tostig arrives at the Humber but is driven out of Yorkshire by Earl Edwin and flees to Scotland.

August: Harald Hardrada's fleet sails from Norway to Orkney.

Late August: William concentrates his fleet and army at the mouth of the river Dives.

September 8: Harold disbands his army.

September 12: William transfers his fleet to St Valery at the mouth of the Somme.

September 20: Battle of Fulford. Edwin and Morcar defeated. Harald Hardrada victorious.

September 24: Harold musters his army at Tadcaster after a rapid march north.

September 25: Battle of Stamford Bridge. Harald Hardrada and Tostig killed. Harold victorious.

September 28-29: William crosses the Channel, landing at Pevensey.

Early October: Harold hears of the Norman landing. William transfers his fleet and army to Hastings.

October 6-11: Harold in London raises a new army.

October 13: Harold's forces rendezvous at the hoar apple tree.

October 14: Battle of Hastings. Harold and his brothers killed. William victorious.

Early December: English leaders submit to William at Berkhamsted.

December 25: William crowned at Westminster.

CAMPAIGNS OF 1066

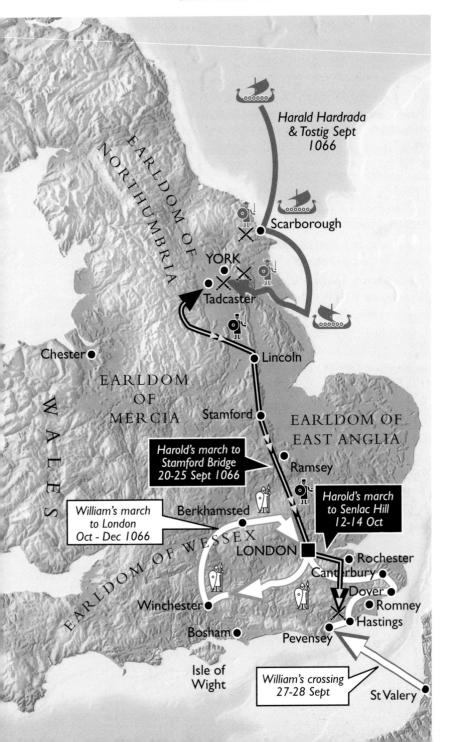

Harald Hardrada & Tostig Sept 1066

EARLDOM OF NORTHUMBRIA

Scarborough

YORK

Tadcaster

Chester

Lincoln

EARLDOM OF MERCIA

WALES

Stamford

EARLDOM OF EAST ANGLIA

Harold's march to Stamford Bridge 20-25 Sept 1066

Ramsey

William's march to London Oct - Dec 1066

Berkhamsted

Harold's march to Senlac Hill 12-14 Oct

EARLDOM OF WESSEX

LONDON

Rochester

Canterbury

Dover

Winchester

Romney

Hastings

Bosham

Pevensey

Isle of Wight

William's crossing 27-28 Sept

St Valery

Chapter 1

1066 – THE BIG THREE

O n 24 April 1066 a comet appeared among the stars. It was Halley's Comet, on one of its regular seventy-five year visits to earth. It remained in the skies for at least a week, shining far more brightly than the feeble display made by the comet on its most recent return, in 1985. Contemporaries described it as a 'hairy star'. In 1066, the meaning of the comet was pondered and debated all over the world, from England to China. Such rare apparitions were regarded as a sign of heavenly wrath, promising some calamity, as Shakespeare reminded us in Julius Caesar:

> When beggars die there are no comets seen:
> The heavens themselves blaze forth the death of princes.

In retrospect, people understood what it had meant. William of Poitiers, our main source for the Battle of Hastings, commented that the comet, 'terror of all kings', which had gleamed so brightly when Harold was newly crowned, was the presage of his defeat and death. On the Bayeux Tapestry, the stylised comet, looking like some strange alien airship, hovers over the palace where King Harold sits uneasily on his throne. Beneath him, in the margin, appears the ghostly outline of ships' hulls, harbingers of the Norman invasion. No words of explanation were offered by the Tapestry's seamstresses, and perhaps none were needed. Harold's calamity was shared by the whole land of England. It was as a result of divine tokens like this the English assumed that God was punishing them for their sins. William of

Halley's Comet blazes in the London skies after Easter 1066. King Harold stirs uneasily on his throne as ghostly ships presage the coming invasion. From the Bayeux Tapestry.

Normandy was merely His instrument.

It is partly this cosmic dimension that makes the year 1066 such a riveting story. In the manner of a classical tragedy, it presents the land being torn apart by one man's error. As a consequence of the breaking of Harold's oath to Duke William, the nation shares in the king's downfall. Of course, this is the story told by the victors, the Normans. Addressing the dead King Harold, William of Poitiers tells him;

> 'you met such success as you deserved, and then, again as you deserved, you met your death, bathed in your own heart's blood ... The cataclysm you caused has dragged you down in its wake. You shine no more beneath the crown you so wrongfully usurped'.

Harold was the last Anglo-Saxon king of England. He reigned for less than a year, from his coronation on 6 January 1066 until his death on the field at Hastings. Although the chronicler John of Worcester claims that Harold 'immediately began to abolish unjust laws and to make good ones', most of his unquiet reign was in fact spent preparing for war and conducting war by land and sea. The poignant single word 'PAX' on the silver pennies of King Harold was only an aspiration. Harold is of course remembered now mainly as the loser of the Battle of Hastings. Until then, however, he had been notably successful in war, having overcome the Welsh in two lightning campaigns, and defeated the last great Viking invasion in a single battle at Stamford Bridge just three weeks before Hastings. Moreover, he was a statesman of experience, having been a great earl for a quarter of a century, first of East Anglia, then of Wessex, and eventually acting as a kind of underking (*subregulus*) as the aging king, Edward the Confessor, became increasingly preoccupied with prayer and hunting.

The story of 1066 is the epic of three men: King Harold and his two great enemies, William, Duke of Normandy and his namesake, Harald Hardrada, Harald the Ruthless, King of

'PAX'. The elegant silver penny of King Harold.

Edward the Confessor.

Norway. It happened because Edward the Confessor died without issue. All three men claimed the throne, Harold with the support of the English nobility, William and Harald by virtue of promises made to them by former kings. Harold's 'war on two fronts' was weakened by divisions at home. His sister was the late king's widow, the dowager Queen Edith, while he and his brothers, the sons of Godwin, were lords of much of England. But their dominance was disputed by a rival family, the sons of Leofric, Edwin and Morcar, who by 1066 ruled the north, having thrown out Harold's brother Tostig the previous year. Despite an arranged marriage between Harold and their sister Aldgyth, tensions between the Houses of Godwin and Leofric were one more factor that determined the way things went in 1066.

Its great men dominate our view of this distant time. We would love to know more about humbler men, for instance Scalpi, Harold's faithful housecarl, or Amund, who was Tostig's, of Hardrada's lieutenants, Stykar and Orri, and Robert de Beaumont, who did so well at Hastings, fighting for Duke William.

King Harold.

Unfortunately they are little more than names. The politics of 1066, as they are presented to us, are the personal contest of two men, Harold and William (with Harald Hardrada opportunistically making trouble from the sidelines). Both were successful rulers in their prime of life, and, despite the passage of nine and a half centuries, something of their presence and personal charisma can still be felt. Let us therefore take a closer look at 'the Big Three' of 1066.

Earl Harold and his brothers

Despite his short reign, we know Harold Godwinson better than any Saxon king since Alfred, thanks to the contemporary tract called the *Vita Ædwardi Regis* (The Life of King Edward). The document, commissioned probably in 1065 by Harold's sister, Queen Edith, was intended to form a eulogy of her family. Its

FAMILY TREES

THE GODWINS

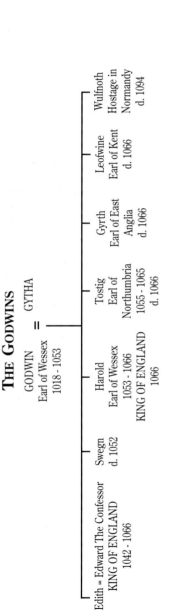

GODWIN
Earl of Wessex
1018 - 1053

=

GYTHA

Edith = Edward The Confessor
KING OF ENGLAND
1042 - 1066

Swegn
d. 1052

Harold
Earl of Wessex
1053 - 1066
KING OF ENGLAND
1066

Tostig
Earl of
Northumbria
1055 - 1065
d. 1066

Gyrth
Earl of East
Anglia
d. 1066

Leofwine
Earl of Kent
d. 1066

Wulfnoth
Hostage in
Normandy
d. 1094

WILLIAM OF NORMANDY

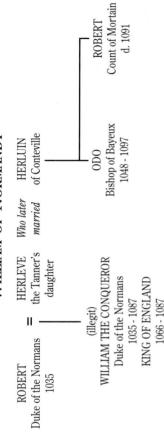

ROBERT
Duke of the Normans
1035

=

HERLEVE
the Tanner's
daughter

*Who later
married*

HERLUIN
of Conteville

(illegit)
WILLIAM THE CONQUEROR
Duke of the Normans
1035 - 1087
KING OF ENGLAND
1066 - 1087

ODO
Bishop of Bayeux
1048 - 1097

ROBERT
Count of Mortain
d. 1091

Harold, the sporting earl, on the way to his family manor at Bosham, Hampshire.

author was a foreign clerk, perhaps from Saint-Omer in what was then Flanders. As it survives, the document is incomplete, but it contains a shrewd and interesting character study of Harold and his younger brother Tostig (the original *Vita* may also have contained a now lost portrait of a third brother, Gyrth), told from a sympathetic but disinterested perspective. Both brothers were serious and responsible men. Though brave, they were not foolhardy, and were capable of disguising their intentions by craft. Harold had the sunnier temperament: he was mild in temper, at ease with himself and others, and could bear contradiction without losing his temper. He was experienced and successful in war, and shrewd in diplomacy. He ruled his great earldom with patience and mercy, showing kindness to all men of good will, but a stern face to evil-doers. Harold was also considered to be something of a statesman, one who had studied the practices of the princes of France and drawn from them knowledge of the management of any business. The portrait is of a good-humoured, intelligent and honourable man, certainly no fool, though perhaps a little too easy-going for his own good. In the next century, the chronicler Orderic Vitalis pays tribute in similar vein to Harold's 'stature and elegance, for his bodily strength, for his quick-wittedness and verbal facility, his sense of humour and his honest bearing'. Harold was a cultivated man; he owned a noted library of books on falconry and so even may have been literate - if so, a most unusual accomplishment for a layman at the time. The author of the Vita sums up the difference between Harold and Tostig thus: 'Harold, aiming at happiness, acted prudently; Tostig, aiming at success, acted vigorously'. Tostig, adds the eulogist, was faithful to his wife and never swore, implying that Harold wasn't, and did.

Tostig was a more steely, puritanical character, secretive, and disinclined to share his plans with others. He 'was stern to law-breakers, and sometimes over-zealous in attacking evil'. He kept his word and never changed his purpose; he was clearly a bad man to cross. Perhaps at the Queen's bidding, the author does his best for Tostig, even at the expense of Harold. For example,

15

Tostig's mission to Rome in 1061 is dealt with at length, whilst an earlier mission of Harold's is dismissed in a few words. The author's main point is that so long as the two brothers remained in amity, England was governed well. It was their quarrel that brought ruin to the land.

After 1066, the Normans, of course, took a more censorious view of Harold. He was an oath-breaker and a man of loose morals, 'a man soiled by luxury, a cruel homicide, proud of his wealth and plunder, an enemy of justice and goodness'. Where Harold was rash, William was prudent, inspired only by thirst for justice. While it suited no one's purpose to denigrate Harold's military prowess, William of Poitiers describes him as Hector to Duke William's Achilles, that is, as a loser who won such measure of success as he merited, and then met a deserved death. But even William of Poitiers pays tribute to Harold's wisdom, courage and strength of will. His badness, it seems, lay mainly in opposing Duke William.

We would like to know what Harold and his brothers looked like and how they bore themselves. While it is useless looking for realistic portraits in the coins and manuscripts of the period, the *Vita* insists that all the Godwins were handsome, graceful men, pleasant to behold. Young Englishmen were famous for being as 'handsome as angels', 'as beautiful as girls'. Re-enactments that show the English with long hair, pig-tails and the rest have got it wrong. Fashionable men wore their hair relatively short, in a pudding-basin style, with shaven chins but long moustaches. William of Malmesbury adds that arms were adorned with gold bracelets, and their skin with 'punctured designs' (i.e. tattoos). Harold's silver penny piece shows the king with a short beard, but this may have been symbolic rather than a portrait. As for the appearance of Harold's brothers, all we know is that Harold was taller than Tostig. Later stories that Harold was unusually tall are unfounded. On the Tapestry, Gyrth is given a long moustache, but the younger Leofwine is cleanshaven, perhaps in allusion to his years (though even Leofwine was past thirty in 1066). Gyrth, it seems, was close to Tostig, Leofwine to Harold. As far as we know, both younger brothers were still bachelors. From scattered hints, fiction writers have tended to portray Gyrth as sober and responsible, Leofwine as amorous and light-spirited. Unlike Tostig, they were loyal and dependable, served the king throughout the campaigns of 1066, and died with him at Hastings.

Until Tostig's disaffection, the Godwins meshed well as a family, ruling most of England as a family partnership. What might have happened if any of the mature Godwin brothers had survived 1066 is one of the endlessly debated 'what-ifs' of history.

Harold's military reputation

Harold had earned a considerable reputation as his country's leading general before 1066; indeed it was probably this above all else that propelled him to the throne. The *Vita* saw him as a second Judas Maccabaeus; he was *'virum fortem et bellicosum'*, a strong and warlike commander. His main war experience was against the Welsh. This was essentially a guerilla war against an elusive enemy who could retreat into the mountains, and emerge to sack a town when the Saxons were looking the other way (Tony Robinson has even suggested that eleventh century Wales was 'our' Afghanistan). In 1055, the Welsh king Gruffydd (pronounced 'Griffith') ap Llywelyn joined forces with the rebellious English earl Aelfgar and attacked Hereford. They defeated the local earl, Ralf, and laid waste the town. Harold led a relief army and fortified Hereford with a deep ditch and gates. Peace was made after Aelfgar was restored to his earldom. But by 1062, the Welsh raids had resumed, and more decisive action was now taken. First Harold nearly captured Gruffydd in a lightning raid on Rhuddlan in north Wales. Then, the following May, Tostig and Harold invaded Wales in a pincer movement, the former attacking the north while Harold's fleet moved along the coast of south Wales, ravaging the countryside and preventing Gruffydd's escape. Finally, the Welsh got rid of Gruffydd themselves, and surrendered his head, along with the gilded prow of his ship, to Harold. Harold took from Gruffydd's successors oaths, confirmed by hostages, that they would be faithful vassals of the king of England. 'After this,' wrote Geoffrey Gaimar, 'no one paid any heed to the Welsh.' It was the great triumph of the age, and contemporaries gave credit to Harold's skill in using picked, lightly-clad mobile units to ravage Wales and defeat any opposition he encountered. While the campaigns proved that Harold was no soft touch, he did show magnanimity to a defeated enemy. Not for 900 years, in the days of Agricola, had Wales been 'so insolently invaded, [and] so easily cowed by force of arms' (Barlow 1970). However, Harold's greatest achievement was not his victory against Gruffydd but the fact that, under the fourteen

The coronation of King Harold by Archbishop Stigand at Westminster Abbey on 6 January 1066.

years of his power, England was more often at peace than at war. And also that, when war came with a vengeance in 1066, it was well prepared.

Earl Harold's claim to the throne

It was the unique circumstances of 1066 that created Harold's opportunity for kingship. Though he was the greatest man in England save only the king, and had, in effect, served as the king's deputy for fourteen years, Harold was a commoner. But King Edward the Confessor died childless in January 1066, and his only close English relative, Edgar Atheling, was still a child. The English faced a choice between Harold, the Duke of Normandy and anarchy. As Professor Alfred Smythe put it in a television programme on King Harold, 'if you were in your right mind it had to be Harold!' There were no voices for Duke William, and the claim of Edgar Atheling was sidelined in the interests of state security. The dying king commended the queen, his servants and all the kingdom to Harold's protection. In the *Vita* he stops short of naming Harold as his heir, but all three Anglo-Saxon chronicles are adamant that he did. The next day Harold was confirmed as King of England by the witan, the Saxon 'parliament'. The English knew Harold's ability and virtues. They believed that only he could unite the English against foreign invasion. Whether Harold connived at the kingship by lobbying or even abusing his paramount position at court, or whether he simply accepted it as his duty, can only be guessed. At any rate, he was the nation's choice. Unfortunately, as the eleventh century saw it, he was not God's choice.

Harald Hardrada and the Norwegian claim

In his obituary of Harald Hardrada, Snorri Sturluson considered that the dead Viking hero surpassed all other men in shrewdness and resource, whether in making instant decisions or long-term plans. He was lucky, as well as brave. He was a generous benefactor to those he liked, and gave gold to poets. Indeed he himself was something of a poet. On the other hand, continues Snorri, God help his enemies. 'The king's guilty men,' wrote one Viking bard; 'pay a heavy penalty. The punishment they receive is earned by their misdeeds: each man gets his due desert. Harald dispenses justice.' His nickname 'Hardrada' means 'hard' or 'ruthless' council. He was an incessant adventurer who delighted in war. He slew his enemies, and dragged their women to his ships in chains. One who had known him said it was appropriate he was killed in another king's land. Physically, Harald Hardrada lived up to his glamorous image. He was exceptionally tall, some said five ells, that is, seven feet six inches. No doubt this was an exaggeration, though King Harold of England allowed him a generous seven feet of Yorkshire earth for his grave. He was a handsome man, of distinguished bearing, with fair hair, a fine beard and long moustaches. He had long, well-shaped hands and feet, and one of his eyebrows was slightly higher than the other, giving him, we might imagine, a 'Roger Moore' look. In 1066 he was aged about fifty.

The Norse king was a living legend. He had been exiled at the tender age of fifteen after the overthrow of his half-brother King Olaf the Saint, and became a freelance warrior with a private army for hire. Enriched by years of successful plundering in Russia and the Mediterranean, he returned to his native land in 1047, and after seven years of civil war, established himself there as king. Harald's claim to the English throne was not very convincing, and largely opportunistic. He seems to have built up support for his candidacy in anti-Godwin parts, notably Mercia and Wales. There is a story that he had been promised the throne by King Harthacnut, but had waived the claim during the lifetime of Harthacnut's successor, Edward the Confessor. Whether he planned to conquer the whole of England in 1066, or just as much of it as he could get his hands on, is uncertain. However, many in England, especially in the north, had strong social ties with Norway and Denmark, and might have preferred the King of Norway to a son of Godwin, especially when they had only just got rid of another of Godwin's boys, Harold's hated brother, Tostig. And Harald Hardrada also drew support from other parts of the British Isles, such as Dublin, Orkney and Viking parts of Scotland. He was, so to speak, the fringe candidate.

Duke William and the Norman claim

A sixteenth century portrait of King William the Conqueror. In fact William was cleanshaven. The art of 1066 did not include recognisable portraits, but the Bayeux Tapestry shows a stocky figure with an intimidating look and pointing gestures that those who knew him might have recognised.

William the Conqueror was another great man who had made his own fortune. As a bastard son of the previous duke and an orphan at the age of twelve, he was lucky to survive the early years of his nominal rule. Three of his guardians were murdered, and there was mayhem in Normandy until 1047, when the young duke managed to rout his enemies at the Battle of Val-ès-Dunes. Thereafter he trounced most of his neighbours in a series of campaigns, not so much by initiating them but by responding aggressively to outside aggression, and beating them at their own game. The impression one receives is one of canniness - William knew when not to fight, as well as when to fight. His success, based on at least a medium-term strategy and sensible decisions, was seen as a sign of God's favour. He was good at fighting, and the reason he was good at it was because he liked it. After the conquest he was flattered as a second Julius Caesar, another Achilles.

William was an impressive man, above average height - he was about five feet nine - and strongly built with a commanding presence. He was personally skilled at arms, a fine horseman and a good shot with a bow. An anonymous monk who knew him remembered his harsh and gutteral voice, but added that he could be fluent and persuasive, 'being skilled at all times in making known his will'. He was said to be abstinent in food and drink, though his corpulence later in life suggests otherwise (on the Tapestry he is consistently shown as a little taller and stouter than Harold. He said his prayers

William, Duke of the Normans, fully armed and carrying his commander's mace.

morning and evening, and was notably faithful to his wife, the diminutive Matilda of Flanders.

William was a master of the brutal arts of eleventh century war, which were about burning, ravaging, pillaging and hostage-taking, as well as occasional fighting. William was a great ravager, as John Gillingham makes clear in his unaffectionate essay, *William the Bastard at War* (reprinted in Murillo, 1996). He ravaged his neighbours, much of England, especially the north, and he was still ravaging when he contracted a fatal illness amid the smouldering embers of Mantes in 1087. At the same time, there are suggestions of a frailer personality inside the 'stern, relentless' warrior and ruler. By returning to Normandy shortly after his coronation, he must have supposed the English had accepted him, and that that was that. The revolutionary nature of the Conquest, its cruelties and dispossessions, it could be argued, was forced on him by the ongoing resistance to his rule - which, in turn, owed much to the racial arrogance of William's followers. In the Conqueror's passion for hunting, David Crouch has sensed a different William, 'a man trapped by duty, by his own inner drive to dominate his world and by the claustrophobia of court life' (Crouch 2002). Crouch's thought-provoking conclusion is that here was a man who, deep down, would rather have been in another job.

Duke William's claim on the throne of England rested on an alleged promise made to him fifteen years earlier. William was cousin, once-removed, to King Edward the Confessor, and there were strong ties of affection and confidence between the courts of England and Normandy. At the high point of Anglo-Norman relations, in 1051, a Norman was even appointed Archbishop of Canterbury. It was then, according to the Normans, that King Edward named the Norman duke as his heir, with the support of

Brothers in arms; Duke William presents Harold with arms after serving together in a campaign against Conan of Brittany in autumn 1064.

his earls. Whether or not he was the sole heir is a different matter. The childless, unworldly king was fickle, and capable of changing his mind. Moreover, Edward had closer relatives than William, including a nephew, Edgar, later named Atheling, meaning he was considered worthy of the throne. The Norman faction at court was overthrown by the Godwins in 1052, when many Normans were expelled. But, in 1064, William strengthened his position by exacting from Harold, the most powerful man in England, an oath to support his claim (see below). By then, William was once again in a strong position by default: his only remaining rival, Edgar Atheling, was a boy, and England had an evil memory of boy-kings. Because he was not of royal line, Harold himself seemed to be ruled out. But in the end, what mattered in 1066 was not right but might. William's claim was 'a fortunate congruence of opportunity, motive and means' (Morillo 1996).

Harold's Oath

The Bayeux Tapestry tells the famous story of Harold's ill-fated expedition to Normandy, of his oath given at Bayeux, his subsequent coronation and his defeat by William at Hastings. It is a moral tale about hubris and the punishment of an oath-breaker. But within the framework of the story, there is a wonderful source of detail on eleventh-century life - of the ships, costumes and arms, buildings, horses, table furnishings, gestures and countless other details. It has scenes that are still moving, despite their stylistic crudity, like the refugee mother and child fleeing from their burning house, or the piggy back rescue of a drowning soldier by Harold, both men hanging on desperately to their shields. Yet, despite all this, the Tapestry is a frustrating document. Restricted to laconic scene 'captions', it does not explain why Harold went to France, nor the nature of the oath he swore. No doubt everyone at Bayeux knew, or thought they knew, just as they knew who 'Wadard', 'Vital' or 'Turold' were, but we never shall, nor will we ever know the meaning of an obscene little figure who appears beneath the picture of 'Aelgyva and a certain clerk'.

Harold's journey took place probably in 1064 (or, less likely, in 1065) when the Earl was at the height of his power. Harold had just decisively overcome years of raiding by the Welsh, and, with his three brothers now full earls, the Godwins were lords of all England except Mercia - the most powerful clan in English history. Why did he go? According to the Norman version of events, Harold was sent to Normandy by King Edward to confirm the king's promise of the succession to Duke William, and to swear allegiance to him. Later chroniclers, notably Eadmer of Canterbury, claimed that the real reason was quite different: Harold had come to secure the release of members of his family held hostage by William, and that his subsequent oath was enforced by blackmail. William of Malmesbury had yet another version. Harold was on a fishing trip, and had been blown across the Channel in a storm. The Bayeux Tapestry, too, seems to tell a different story, for, whatever the nature of the oath Harold swore, he is shown on his return in a posture of humility, being roundly rebuked for it by King Edward. Moreover, on his deathbed, the

Harold swears his forced oath of allegiance on the relics of the saints under the eyes of the Duke and his court. William appears solemn and majestic, Harold seems cornered and anxious.

A nineteenth-century engraving showing Harold swearing an oath to the Duke of Normandy.

king holds out his hand to Harold, indicating his assent to Harold's claim to the throne. There is no doubt that whatever Edward may have promised to Duke William fifteen years before, he named Harold his successor in 1066.

The Tapestry starts with the scene in which Harold is being instructed by King Edward, but to what end we are not told. Next, in a series of delightful scenes of eleventh-century sporting life, Harold and his retinue ride to his family seat at Bosham, near Chichester. He evidently enjoyed some hunting on the way, for belled hounds run before him, and he holds a hawk on his wrist. After prayers at Bosham church, there is a gratuitous drinking scene in the hall. The next day Harold, still holding his hawk, boards a ship. Two of his men carry fishing poles - is this the origin of Malmesbury's story? Under full sail in a choppy sea, but with no sign of a storm, they land on the coast of Ponthieu where Harold and his party are arrested by the local count. Harold resists: when seized he pulls a knife, but his party are overcome and taken as prisoners to Count Guy's castle at Beaurain.

The scene then shifts to the court of Duke William of Normandy where messengers arrive in haste to tell him what has happened. William himself sets out, meeting Count Guy and ordering him in no uncertain terms to hand over Harold and his party. Harold appears again, still with his hawk, while in the lower border, apparently irrelevantly, a naked couple are about to embrace. This is probably a sly reference to Harold's lechery. Elsewhere, peacocks, pelicans and beasts devouring their own tails seem to hint at other unfavourable aspects of Harold, respectively symbols of pride, perjury and vainglory. There is also a tiny figure of a naked man building what looks like a coffin - perhaps a hint that Harold is digging his own grave. Harold is taken to William's palace at Rouen and treated as an honoured guest. He is the Duke's companion on campaign against Count Conan of Brittany, and distinguishes himself by rescuing two Normans from quicksands. On their return, William ceremoniously presents Harold with arms, including a banner. By this ritual, Harold has agreed to enter the Duke's service. Next, in the presence of William, comes the fatal oath, with Harold poised like a disc jockey, his outstretched arms touching two holy reliquaries. William's nobles point to the word 'SACRAMENTUM' to signify the solemnity of the event, but the nature of the oath is not enlarged upon. Then Harold sails home to England, to what is obviously a chilly reception at the court of Edward the Confessor. Shortly afterwards, Edward dies and Harold is acclaimed king, thus breaking his oath to William. Almost immediately a 'long-haired star' - Halley's comet - appears in the sky, a sign, in retrospect at least, of God's anger.

What did Harold promise, and why did he agree to something so harmful to his own prospects? When informed people, even at the time, were in disagreement about what had gone on, there can be no certainty from nearly a thousand years away. The traditional story is at least consistent. If King Edward sent Harold to Normandy to confirm William's succession, then the rest of the story falls into place logically. It has been suggested that Harold might even have taken an oath of fealty to William willingly on the understanding that he would act as an 'underking' in England while William was away. It would not be a bad deal from his point of view, and would preserve Godwin power. On the other hand, there were no voices for William in England, and Harold might well have injured his standing by becoming the duke's man. And everything we know of Harold suggests he was a patriot who put his country first, even at the expense of his own family. More likely the oath was made under duress, and that Harold had no intention of keeping it. Perhaps it was made a condition of the release of the hostages, or even of Harold himself. However, the most important hostage, Harold's youngest brother, Wulfnoth, remained in William's hands (as he was to do for the rest of his life). Harold was only allowed to take with him an unnamed nephew (*nepos*), probably Hakon, the son of his dead brother Sweyn.

What exactly was the oath? According to William of Poitiers, Harold had sworn to represent the Duke's interests in England, and work for his succession. This is probably more or less true. He also agreed to hand over the town of Dover and certain estates to William as a pledge of good conduct. This is less likely, for this would not have been within Harold's gift. Harold was made to swear on certain holy relics. This was especially damaging, since breaking such an oath was regarded as a serious crime and an offence before God. It was also a grave hostage to fortune, since, if Harold broke his promise, William could, and did, present him to the courts of Europe as a perjurer as well as a vassal. This is why the oath scene is the fulcrum of the story told on the Bayeux Tapestry. It presents the classic tragedy of the downfall of a man brought down by one mistake. From then on, Harold was morally damaged.

Chapter 2

1066 – A GUIDE TO THE SOURCES

The mind-world of 1066

The England of 1066 was surprisingly cosmopolitan. For the past half-century its rulers had been Danish (Canute and his two short-lived sons) or half-Norman (Edward the Confessor's mother was a Norman princess, and the king himself had spent his formative years at the Norman court). England was part of the cultural and political world of northern Europe. Favoured figures at court included Normans, Danes and Icelandics. All the principal characters of 1066 had seen something of the world, most notably Harald Hardrada, but both Harold and Tostig had led diplomatic missions to Rome and Flanders. England was famous for its wealth, founded in agriculture, and had a more or less ordered system of local administration. The state had recovered from the Danish wars earlier in the century, and people seem to have regained confidence in themselves. There was a growing sense of nationhood. It took the Conqueror nearly ten years after Hastings to overcome resistance to his rule, and the stubbornness of the English evidently took him and his advisers by surprise.

An eighteenth century engraver's portrait of Canute, loosely based on his coinage.

This world had two contrasting sets of heroes. The first were the saints. God's kingdom felt close in 1066: the world of the hereafter was as real and present as the physical one. Homilies on the lives of the saints, and moral precepts drawn from them, was one strand of Saxon literature. The other great source of inspiration was the man of action, the war-leader, exemplified above all by the Vikings. There were even heroes that fulfilled both roles, like Olaf Haraldson, Harald Hardrada's half-brother, fellow king and martyred saint, whose sanctity took the form of severely punishing those who disobeyed him by refusing compulsory baptism! It is through the surviving stories and sagas that one can peer slightly beneath the surface of the eleventh century world. The culture was simple, vigorous and masculine. Traditional values were the only values. Ideals and codes of behaviour were essentially military, shaped by comradeship and shared danger. At the Battle of Hastings, some might have remembered the words of Brightwold at the Battle of Maldon, seventy years earlier: 'Thoughts must be the braver, hearts the more valiant, courage the greater, as our strength grows less'. In the sagas, collected and written down by Snorri Sturluson, history is strongly dramatised, and designed to be heard rather than read. The poet needed to entertain his audience. Poetic convention demanded that hero-kings like Harald Hardrada become personifications of bravery, forever scourging their enemies and pursuing fame and power. Snorri's Viking audience expected an 'upbeat' story of adventure and uncomplicated valour. There was, one imagines, a lot of audience participation. There is little history in the modern sense in Snorri's tales - no analysis of why things went the way they did, no examination of character and motive. This is the world of the simple comic-book hero, a kind of early medieval Hollywood, or Harald Hardrada meets the Brothers Grimm. In the eleventh century, history very quickly turned into verse and song. In a sense there was no history, only a kind of tale telling in which the facts were adapted to the versifier's design. The audience honoured losers as well as winners. For example, it held Byrtnoth, the leader at Maldon, in high regard, even though he lost the battle. It was not the winning that mattered so much as how you played the game. Losing with style is among the oldest English traditions.

Behind the glory-seeking, this world seems static and distinctly sad. There is no romance and love interest in the sagas, though there is eroticism. There is a recognition that life is hard, beastly and often short (not one Saxon king in the 150 years between Alfred and Edward the Confessor reached old age). Man must endure. At work in eleventh century minds was the tension between the teaching of the Church, that man must prepare on earth for everlasting life in the next world, with the antithetical pagan view that immortality meant fame in this world. Saints looked over one shoulder, saga heroes the other.

The Norman chroniclers belong to a different literary tradition, one designed to be read by educated people rather than listened to in a smoky hall. It does not necessarily make them more reliable. Poets needed to be careful, since misrepresenting the facts would risk insulting someone in the audience, perhaps with violent consequences. But chroniclers can provide detail and subtlety of argument that the poet could not, helped by the fact that their language was classical Latin rather than an essentially oral language like Old English. The chroniclers had their own conventions, and William of Poitiers in particular makes frequent reference to the great men of Greece and Rome. It was important for his purposes to glorify Duke William as a superhero, a second Julius Caesar. The Norman conquerors also needed historians to dignify their past and underline their sense of destiny. Soon after 1066, the monk William of Jumièges obliged with an eight-book epic on the great deeds of the dukes, starting with the mythical founder, prophetically called Hastingus, and ending with the Battle of Hastings and the coronation of King William. The Normans, like the English, were the prisoners of convention. Just as Achilles personally slew Hector in *The Iliad*, so Guy of Amiens has Harold slaying his brother Tostig, and, later on, represents Duke William slaying Harold's other brother, Gyrth, before going on to lead the assault on Harold himself! More importantly, none of them showed much interest in the other side; their job was to cheer on the winners.

Culturally the leading men of 1066 had much in common (William and Harold evidently got on famously during the latter's enforced stay in Normandy in 1064). But they were not alike. On the Bayeux Tapestry, the manners and gestures of the English and the Normans are shown in interesting contrast. While Harold and his party appear as easy-going, amiable and slightly foppish, Duke William and his court have an altogether steelier look to go with their short hair and martial bearing. William points; orders are obeyed, boats are built and loaded with logistical efficiency, the knights stand proudly in their high-pommelled saddles. Only in the battle itself do the two sides show similar focus and determination. We might deduce from the subsequent reigns of the Norman kings that the Norman aristocracy was still rough-edged, arrogant and inclined to see itself as a superior race. Harold has his library, his hawks, his family life. But William and his knights are rarely glimpsed away from the business of war and conquest, except when at prayer or out hunting. One is left with a sense of a rather dreamy, complacent England, comfortable in its

English informality and facial hair. (Left) contrasted with (right) Norman formality and crew-cuts but are those ear rings?

This contemporary illustration shows how the Normans were viewed: determined, disciplined and focused in combat. This is a rare view of Norman infantry, almost completely lacking on the Bayeux Tapestry.

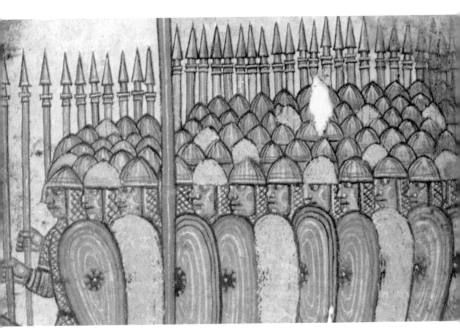

past, and a people across the Channel with a different worldview, a sense that they were going forward to greatness and for whom the pursuit of fame and wealth was more than a game.

The Sources

Why has there not been an epic film of 1066 to rival, say, *Spartacus* or *Cleopatra*? (for that matter, why didn't Shakespeare write a play about it?). The drama is ready made, with a tragic hero (Harold), a bitter and twisted rival (Tostig) and a hard man with his eye on the ball (William). For the climactic battle scene, we are far better off for Hastings than Shakespeare's Bosworth or Hollywood's *Spartacus* battles. For Hastings we have three strictly contemporary accounts, more than a dozen slightly later ones, and, uniquely, a 'strip cartoon' of the battle and episodes leading up to it in the Bayeux Tapestry. Everyone alive then and for long afterwards recognised its importance. The chroniclers of a generation later saw 1066 as the start of a new period in English history, and retrospected in some detail, probably using sources which are now lost to us. Historians, too, have always found it a fascinating year. The starting point is the Scottish philosopher David Hume's monumental *History of England* (1754-62). The classic nineteenth century version is E.A. Freeman's impassioned and minutely documented *History of the Norman Conquest* (1873). Freeman's championship of King Harold and traditional Saxon values began a feud with Norman historians, exemplified by J.H. Round, which continued through the twentieth century. Classic accounts of our own time include General Fuller's masterly summary in his *Decisive Battles of the Western World*, Sir Frank Stenton's in his standard textbook, *Anglo-Saxon England*, and Colonel Alfred Burne's field-based tour in his *Battlefields of England*. More recently M.K. Lawson (2002) offers a comprehensive treatment summarising all the sources as well as the most minute examination of the battlefield. There were at least four television documentaries on the events of 1066 broadcast in a single year between 2002-2003, each claiming it had new evidence to reveal: (new speculations maybe; new evidence, hardly). The most exciting accounts are in fiction: in *The Golden Warrior* (1949) by Hope Muntz and *The Last English King* (1997) by Julian Rathbone, both of which give a stronger impression of what the battle might have been like than any 'academic' reconstruction.

None of these authors discovered new sources for the battle. The last major source to turn up was the *Carmen* or Song of the Battle of Hastings, discovered in 1826, but not committed to print until 1840. What the writers in the half-century after 1066 had to say about it could be contained in a book the size of a paperback novel. Stephen Murillo's indispensible book on Hastings (Murillo 1996) includes edited translations of the six main primary sources. Unfortunately this does not mean one can approach the Battle of Hastings in the same way as the Napoleonic wars or twentieth century campaigns. The sources tell different stories, and they are often muddled and hard to interpret. The language of the eleventh century used rhetoric for poetic effect. For example, the long speeches attributed to Duke William are a convenient way of summarising the situation as he might have seen it. There is, unfortunately, no 'perfect' source for Hastings, nor indeed for any other medieval battle. William of Poitiers' *Gesta Willelmi* is the nearest thing to a standard account, but his purpose was not to analyse the battle disinterestedly but to praise the greatest of all the great deeds of Duke William with all the rhetoric and exaggeration at his command. Already, with all the advantages of nearness in time and close acquaintance with its hero, the battle is presented as if through stained glass. The process is taken further in the *Carmen*: though it is vivid and circumstantial, poetry often triumphs over fact. One has a sense that both authors were writing with one eye on what boastful knights had told them, and the other on a copy of Homer, outspread on their knees. Probably the least biased of the sources is the Bayeux Tapestry, but even that is essentially the Norman version, may not be trustworthy in all its detail, and poses more questions than it answers. The greatest drawback of all is that we do not have an adequate account of the battle from the English viewpoint. To the victor go the spoils! - and they include the writing of history.

Popular accounts of the Battle of Hastings tend to pick and mix among the sources to produce a lively, coherent narrative. But blow-by-blow accounts of the battle are a matter of interpretation; the facts do not always help us much. For example, we know something about the opening and the final moments of the battle, but very little idea about what went on between noon and late afternoon! On the English side, we know little or nothing about who stood where, except that Harold was roughly in the middle (and we don't know what Harold did either, before he was cut down by the fatal arrow). Sometimes, where the sources are contradictory, writers simply lump one story with another. For example, for the climactic scene - the death of King Harold - the story of the arrow is combined with another involving four knightly assassins. Though it makes a great narrative, it isn't one that anyone told at the time, but rather the unwarranted splicing together of two different tales, neither of which may be true!

Similarly, the sources have a lot to say about William the warrior, but less about William the commander. Writers tend to accept at face value the literary sources' view of William as being in the thick of the fighting, but they ignore the contrary evidence of the Tapestry, where William is never in the front line, lacks a shield, and wields nothing more fearful than his wooden *baculum* of office. In truth, enough can be construed from the sources to reconstruct the basic lineaments of the battle, but the effect is like coarse newsprint: the closer you look, the less you see. The historiography of the battle is based on tendentious stories and anecdotes, some probably more or less true, some exaggerated, and some invented. The Battle of Hastings we know is probably an approximation of what actually happened, but we see it from a distance, and through a canon of writing that aimed at effect rather than fact.

The most detailed account of the Battle of Hastings is the *Gesta Willelmi*, The Deeds of William, by William of Poitiers. The full title is *Gesta Willelmi ducis Normannorum et regis Ænglorum*, the deeds of William, duke of the Normans and king of the English. The author was a Norman who knew the duke well, and had served him first as a soldier and later as his chaplain. He wrote the *Gesta* in the 1070s, by which time William of Poitiers had become the Archdeacon of Lisieux. Although he did not accompany the duke to Hastings, William of Poitiers had access to some who had, and his account must therefore rest on eye-witness testimony, not least from Duke William himself. But even so, the author was guided by what he had read and admired in the writings of the ancient world, and in the battle scenes uses rhetoric, often to muddled effect. His William can do no wrong, and his English are little more than arrow fodder. Modern readers of the *Gesta Willelmi* will not miss what Eric John has called 'the arrogance of success and the brutality of triumph' (John 1982).

The *Carmen de Hastingae Proelio* or Song of the Battle of Hastings is equally dramatic, full of circumstantial information like weather reports, that again suggest eyewitness testimony. In form it is a long Latin poem in praise of the victors at Hastings. Professor Frank Barlow makes a convincing case that it is the work of Bishop Guy of Amiens, a cousin of one of the leaders at Hastings, and written within a few years of the battle. An opposing view, led by the late Professor R.H.C. Davis, that it is, rather, a late literary compilation from the early years of the next century, and so of little independent value has gone out of fashion. Bishop Guy was a member of the ruling family of Ponthieu, and, as one would expect, emphasises the contribution of Ponthieu to the final victory. The role of the French and the Bretons is also talked up, while there is a definite dig at the Normans, fleeing from English peasants 'with their shields on their backs'! A modern reader of the *Carmen* may be surprised at the bloodthirstiness displayed by an eleventh century bishop.

The *Anglo-Saxon Chronicle* is the best English source we have for 1066. Three different verions, known as 'C', 'D' and 'E' survive. All view the events of the year as disastrous, but only 'D' devotes much attention to Hastings, while 'C' and 'E' are more interested in events 'up north', including York and Stamford Bridge. Between them, they cover the events of that calamitous year tersely but offer some valuable straws from the English perspective, such as Harold's unpreparedness at Hastings. The chronicle of 'Florence' of Worcester (now more usually referred to as John of Worcester), though compiled in the early twelfth century, may have used a lost version of the *Anglo-Saxon Chronicle*. He is one of the 'big four' twelfth century chronicles: the others being by William of Malmesbury, Henry of Huntingdon and Orderic Vitalis, all clerical writers more or less sympathetic to the English. They all offer interesting views on 1066, some of them contradictory, and are probably a blend of fact and fiction. The challenge to any historian is to sort the wheat from the chaff.

Another source is the *Gesta Normannorum Ducum* (Deeds of the Dukes) of William of Jumièges, which was supplemented later on by Orderic Vitalis and Robert of Torigni. Considering its early date, written within a few years of 1066, it is disappointingly brief on the Battle of Hastings. The relevant part of the chronicle may be missing. Orderic adds some vivid snippets, like the piles of bones at Stamford Bridge, and his probably more accurate version of the Malfosse incident.

There is some additional material in the eleventh century writings of Baudri de Bourgeuil, who was one of the first to claim that Harold was slain by an arrow. Another, writing about sixty years after the battle, is Geoffrey Gaimar, a secular clerk from Lincolnshire, whose *History of the English* (written in French) contains romanticised stories about Hastings, perhaps based on songs and other oral tradition. He is notably well-informed on northern matters, and knew how many ships Harald Hardrada had, and, uniquely, how many counties were represented at the Battle of Fulford. Another source is the *Chronicle of Battle Abbey* which, in addition to much legendary material, helps to identify the battlefield and has some unique information about Harold's famous oath.

No source has had a greater impact on the popular view of the Battle of Hastings than the Bayeux Tapestry. The seventy metre-long (230 feet) embroidery, which has been among the possessions of the Cathedral of Bayeux since at least 1476, is believed to have been designed and executed in the 1070s at St Augustine's Abbey in Canterbury as a commission for William's half-brother, Odo, by now earl of Kent as well as Bishop of Bayeux. The Tapestry illustrates the official story of Harold's disastrous journey, of his enforced stay as guest of Duke William and of the oath he took at Bayeux. Its broad message is that Harold betrayed his feudal lord, William, by accepting the English crown, and so received his comeuppance at Hastings. Although the full import of the oath is not spelled out, scenes in the borders hint at Harold's treachery and lasciviousness, as well as his troubled conscience. The Bayeux Tapestry flatters Bishop Odo and his brother the duke, and subtly undermines Harold by, for example, showing the excommunicate prelate, Stigand, presiding at his coronation. The missing section, at the end probably culminated in William's coronation at Westminster. The Tapestry's main value lies in its pictorial detail. For anyone who likes lists, it contains 626 people, 190 horses and mules, 35 dogs, 506 other animals, 33 buildings, 37 ships and 37 trees. Without these 'strip cartoons', we would have little idea of what the men of 1066 looked like and how they lived.

Of the late sources, the most interesting is the *Roman de Rou* (the history of Rollo) by Robert Wace, a verse chronicle written nearly a century after the battle. Wace, a native of Jersey, was canon of Bayeux, and obviously well-versed in the traditions of 1066. It is from Wace that we have such details as the name of William's messenger to Harold, his prefabricated fort at Hastings, and the exact number of ships that took William's army across the Channel. In Wace's account, a prominent role is given to Harold's brother Gyrth. The Victorian historian E.A. Freeman made free use of Wace, but modern historians tend to regard him as essentially an elaborator, with little fresh evidence to add. A further problem is that the full transcript of the *Roman de Rou* is available only in the original French. That something may be lost in translation is suggested by this little gem, obviously current in twelfth century Bayeux:

> 'The arrow which struck Harold's eye
> Was straight and strong. Down from the sky
> It screamed, delighting all the French
> Who cheered to see blind Harold blench.'

The sign of the Swordsman Inn at Stamford Bridge celebrating the famous, but probably fictitious, Viking champion who held the Saxon army at bay.

Because the Norman and French chroniclers knew or cared little about them, the Battles of Fulford and Stamford Bridge are much more poorly documented. The Bayeux Tapestry completely ignores Harold's northern campaign. The main sources: the *Anglo-Saxon Chronicle*, especially the 'C' and 'E' chronicles, the Chronicle of John of Worcester and King Harald's Saga from the *Heimskringla* by the Icelandic bard, Snorri Sturluson. The famous story of the brave 'berserker' who held up the English army at Stamford Bridge is unfortunately not in the original *Anglo-Saxon Chronicle*, but added a century later. There are also snippets from later chronicles, notably, Symeon of Durham, Marianus

36

Scotus and Geoffrey Gaimer, though they may not be very reliable.

Snorri is the only author to provide details of the fighting. His story is lively, almost like a novel in places, but, being written long after the event, is more of a work of poetry than of history. It shows how Harald Hardrada's ill-fated invasion was remembered, 170 years later, and probably incorporates oral history, sung in praise of the great, if ruthless, Norse hero. Some things he gets wrong - like the supposed death of Morcar at Fulford and the fictitious English cavalry charge at Stamford Bridge. But others, like the English spears 'sparkling like a field of broken ice', have an authentic ring to them.

In summary, the main primary sources for the campaigns of 1066 are as follows:

The Gesta Guillelmi of William of Poitiers, edited and translated by R.C.H. Davis and M. Chibnall (Oxford Medieval Texts, 1988). The chapters on the Battle of Hastings are printed in full in Murillo (1996) and Thorpe (1973).

The *Carmen de Hastingae Proelio* of Guy, bishop of Amiens. Edited and translated by Frank Barlow (Oxford Medieval Texts; 1999). Also reprinted in Murillo (1996).

The Bayeux Tapestry. There are scholarly editions by Sir Frank Stenton: *The Bayeux Tapestry: a Comprehensive Survey.* (Phaidon, 1965) and by Sir David Wilson: *The Bayeux Tapestry* (Thames & Hudson, 1985). There are many other edited reproductions, e.g. Thorpe (1973), Rud (1988).

The Anglo-Saxon Chronicle. Edited by Dorothy Whitelock, David Douglas and S.I. Tucker. (Eyre & Spottiswade, 1961). A new edition is in preparation from Cambridge University Press. I have used the Everyman's Library translation by G.N. Garmonsway (1954).

King Harald's Saga. In Book III of Snorri Sturluson's *Heimskringla*, translated with introduction by Magnus Magnusson and N. Palsson (Penguin Books, 1966).

Other primary sources:

The Gesta Normannorum Ducum of William of Jumièges, Orderic Vitalis and Robert of Torigni, edited and translated by E.M.C. Van Houts in two volumes (Oxford Medieval Texts, 1992, 1995). The relevant passages are all in the seventh book.

The Life of King Edward who rests at Westminster (Vita

Aedwardi Regis), edited and translated by Frank Barlow (Oxford Medieval Texts, 1992).

The *Chronicle of John of Worcester*, vol. 2, edited by R.R. Darlington and P. McGurk (Oxford Medieval Texts, 1995).

De Gestis regum Anglorum of William of Malmesbury, edited and translated by R.A.B. Mynors, R.M. Thompson and M. Winterbottom (Oxford Medieval Texts, 1998).

Historia Ecclesiastica of Orderic Vitalis, edited and translated in six volumes by M. Chibnall (Oxford Medieval Texts, 1969-80).

The *Historia Anglorum* of Henry of Huntingdon, edited and translated by D. Greenway (Oxford Medieval Texts, 1996).

Le Roman de Rou of Robert Wace of Bayeux. French text, edited by A.J. Holden, (Sociètè des anciens textes francais, 1970-73).

'*Chronicle of Battel Abbey*'. *The Brevis relatio de Guillelmo nobilissimo comite Normannorum written by a Monk of Battle Abbey*, edited by E.M.C. Van Houts (Camden Society, 1997).

L'Estoire des Engleis of Geoffrey Gaimar. Edited and translated by Sir T.D. Hardy and C.T. Martin (Rolls Series, 91, 1988-89).

Chapter 3

ARMS AND ARMOUR

Swords

The sword (Old English: *sweord*) was the weapon of highest status in 1066, passed from one generation to the next as an heirloom. For example, King Æthelred's son, who predeceased him, left his father a precious 'silver-hilted sword' which in turn had once belonged to an earl called Ulfkell. Swords were often given names. In old English literature swords are variously described as 'brand flame', 'battle-friend', 'treasure-sword' and 'slaughter-knife'. A typical eleventh century sword was slightly tapering, double-edged and broad-bladed with a shallow groove running along the centre to reduce its weight. The crossguards were generally short and stubby, and curved away from the hand. The pommel was large, often D-shaped, like a tea cosy, or lobed. The grip was probably covered with padded leather, though this is never preserved. The hilts of expensive swords were inlaid with silver or gilded, and ornately decorated. This was a weapon designed for hacking and slashing. Swords were wielded in one hand, while the other held a shield to defend the body. They were a particularly effective cavalry weapon, the knight using the extra height to slice or hack blows onto the heads of foot soldiers. On the Bayeux Tapestry, sword blows are usually swung overhead from the shoulder. Blows are often aimed at the head - and there is confirmation of this in burials from the period, where sheared skulls are not infrequent. The sword could also be used defensively, by parrying a blow, holding the hilt high with the blade slanted across the body. However the lack of 'edge damage' on medieval swords suggests that the 'thrust-and-parry' of the Robin Hood films was fiction. If the swordsman failed to land his blow, he would either have got out of the way quickly, or turned so that the shield took the force of his opponents' counter-blow. A direct hit to the head would disable a man, helmet or no helmet, and might even break his neck - heavy eleventh century swords were effectively clubs as well as cutting tools. In the Sagas, at least, expert swordsmen used a second sword in lieu of a shield.

The best swords were made by a process known as 'pattern-welding'. The idea was to make the blade more supple and

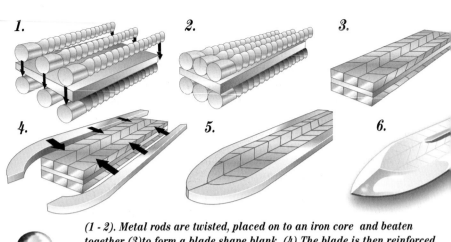

(1 - 2). Metal rods are twisted, placed on to an iron core and beaten together (3)to form a blade shape blank. (4) The blade is then reinforced with mild steel sides and tip. (6) The sides and tip are then honed to form the cutting edge and point of the sword.

Left: An eleventh century Anglo-Saxon sword with a 'tea-cosy' pommel, broad blade and 'trademark'.

resilient by forging together iron and mild steel. Briefly, metal rods were twisted together and welded by the swordsmith into a blade-shaped blank. Further treatment produced a flat, springy blade bearing a characteristic herringbone patterning, the result of welding rods with varying carbon content. The process spread the carbon content of mild steel evenly throughout the blade, so strengthening the sword and making it shatterproof. The blade was then reinforced with a steel shoe, added to the sides and tip, and then honed to form the cutting edge and point. Of course, the process was slow and time-consuming, and was the work of a skilled metalsmith. Expert swordsmiths sometimes left their names in the blade as a trademark. Ulfberht was one of them, perhaps the Saxon equivalent of a Stradivarius violin or a Chippendale chair. Only the finest swords received the undiluted attention of the Ulfberhts. Cheaper (but still expensive) swords were mass-manufactured in large workshops, to standard designs. A still cheaper form of sword was the seax, with only one cutting edge, and presumably used

Right: The seax, a cheap and mass produced sword used by foot-soldiers.

like an axe, or, attached to a large haft, as a poleaxe.

Swords were carried in wooden scabbards, lined outside with leather and inside with wool or fur to keep the blade oiled and rust-free. Some scabbards were decorated with beads or rock crystal. By 1066, most were worn on a waist belt, though in earlier times they had been worn higher, attached to a shoulder strap or baldric. Evidently the belt and scabbard were worn beneath mail, with the hilts protruding from a pocket at the side.

Did all the 'officer class' carry swords? The Tapestry shows many men on both sides apparently without swords or scabbards. Leofwine and Harold have scabbards, but Gyrth has none, and neither have some of the spear-throwers in the shieldwall. Perhaps some warriors preferred to unstrap their heavy swords and cumbrous scabbards before going into close combat with spears and axes. Or perhaps, in some cases, the tapestry designer simply forgot to add a scabbard!

Shields

Shields were born both by mounted and foot-soldiers in 1066, although English axemen, and possibly some swordsmen, did without, relying on a companion shield-bearer for protection.

Norman 'kite' shield.

Two kinds of shields were in use in 1066. The latest type was the narrow, tapering kite shield, which ran down the length of the body from neck to ankle, and, in effect, was an extension of body armour. The kite shield may have been a Norman cavalry fashion adopted by the English. The other type is like a buckler or 'target', round and

'Target' shield.

Norman knights carrying kite-shaped shields always on the left arm by a cross-ways bar or strap.

Eleventh century shields often carried distinctive devices like these winged dragons carried by two of William's emissaries. Though not heraldic in the formal sense, they probably helped identify the bearers.

heavier, with a central iron boss. It was used to cover the body in close quarter fighting, and to push or bludgeon one's opponent. Both kinds were in use at Hastings. Richard Glover has plausibly suggested that the more primitive round shields were plundered from the Vikings after Stamford Bridge to replace English ones damaged in battle.

Shields were made from wooden planks covered by cowhide leather. The latter, when applied wet, will shrink tight onto the wooden boards, holding the shield together and (after dubbing) making it weatherproof. The shield was shaped by steaming and bending the wood over a mould. Because it needed to be strong yet supple, and withstand repeated blows, shields were probably made by gluing or riveting together strips of cross-plyed wood of different grains. The edges would be reinforced with leather or metal. The frequent mention of 'lindenwood' (i.e. limewood) shields in Saxon poetry is not born out by archaeological evidence. In Saxon weapon burials, alder and willow are the shield-woods of choice, followed by maple and birch. What shields were *not* made of is oak and ash. Despite their strength, these woods are heavy, and too prone to split.

Shields were grasped by an iron bar rivetted to the inside, clearly shown on the Bayeux Tapestry. To secure the forearm they also had either a leather strap or a square of straps for forearm and hand, probably resting on a pad to cushion the force of a blow. When not in use, the shield could be slung over the back by a strap.

The shields of Hastings bear an interesting range of patterns or 'devices', from geometrical arrangements of bosses and rivets, to cross-shaped bands and even stylised beasts. King Harold's 'device' was an ornate cross, while Earl Gyrth's shield was an old-fashioned round one, heavily studded with a sharp central spike. These devices were not heraldic in the later sense, but they were clearly designed for recognition and may have been the emblem of a particular family or faction. Later legend claims that Duke William bore two leopards or lions, a prototype of the lions of England.

The shield was central to the English way of fighting. At Maldon, and again at Hastings, a defensive wall of shields protected the front line of warriors. At Maldon, Ealderman Byrhtnoth bade his men hold their shields 'in the right way, firm with the fist, and have no fear'. Losing a shield in battle was considered more shameful than losing a sword. After a long battle like Hastings, many shields must have been in a terrible state, hacked and battered, with arrows sticking through.

Mail

By the time of Hastings, those that could afford to fought in body armour and a helmet. This may have been a fairly recent innovation. In the past, chainmail or even the cheaper version, 'fishscale' armour, seems to have been used only by the wealthiest, and even then as a short 'shirt' rather than a longer 'coat'. Mail is not even mentioned in the epic poem, *The Battle of Maldon*, composed about

Chain mail links.

seventy years earlier (though it may have been taken for granted). Mail corrodes easily and has rarely survived. Almost the only examples from the Saxon period are from Coppergate in tenth century York, and from the warrior's grave at Sutton Hoo in the seventh century. Judging from these, mail was made from rings a quarter of an inch in diameter, in rows alternatively rivetted and hammered together for added strength and flexibility. A coat of mail would weigh about thirty pounds, depending on length, light enough for a horse to carry without tiring, and also supple and flexible. Only a couched lance driven home by a charging horse, or a well-aimed arrow at close range, could penetrate it.

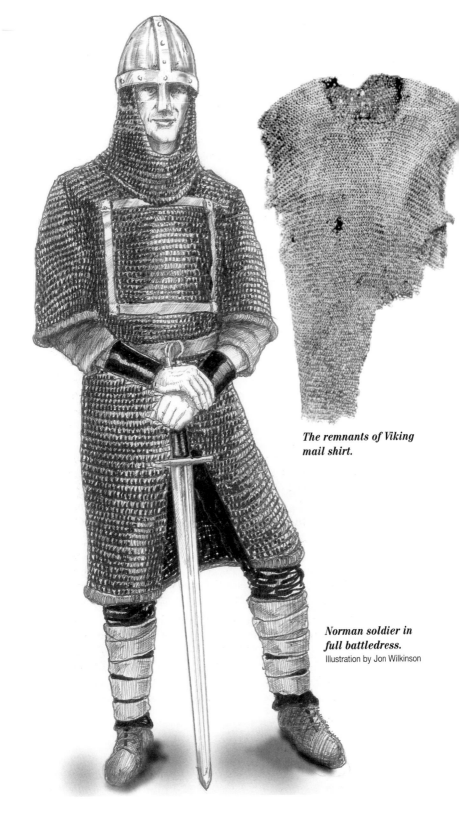

The remnants of Viking mail shirt.

Norman soldier in full battledress.
Illustration by Jon Wilkinson

Mail was heavy. William of Poitiers has an anecdote about William the Conqueror, who gained great credit by carrying the mail of a companion on his shoulder while wearing his own. The mailshirts worn by the English are referred to as byrne or byrnies, while the Norman mail is normally called a hauberk. Despite this linguistic difference, judging from the Bayeux Tapestry the mail worn on either side was remarkably similar. Most warriors wear a hooded, short-sleeved, knee-length coat of mail, split at the front and rear for riding and easier movement. A few Normans, including Duke William and Count Eustace, also wear mail sleeves and leggings. So does Earl Harold on the occasion of his knighting by William, but not on the battlefield at Hastings. Mail was trimmed along the hems with leather. A prominent square of leather straps across the chest worn only by Normans is usually interpreted as a loose ventail, a flap to guard the throat. It certainly seems to disappear when the knights are 'zipped up' ready for combat, but as shown it seems too bulky for this purpose. Perhaps instead the straps held in place a cushioned pad worn underneath the mail.

The lower parts of the arms and legs were normally protected by bands of material, probably of boiled leather, rather like modern puttees. Evidently neither side wore protective mittens nor gloves, and the feet were shod in short leather shoes rather than high boots. Beneath the mail, men wore a leather or quilted tunic to help absorb a blow.

No doubt the knight's servants kept his mail well-polished and free from rust. In the next century, mail was sometimes known as 'white harness' from its silver shimmer. Mail was valuable. In the later stages of the battle, the Tapestry margins are crowded with small folk pulling off the hauberks and byrnies of the fallen. Off the battlefield, the Norman knights wore tunics, shown on the Tapestry by crosshatching instead of rings. This was presumably a lighter, quilted form of armour, worn on the march, and when out foraging. Some of the English in the shieldwall also wear this form of crosshatched protection. It has also been interpreted as fishscale armour, in which bits of metal, horn or leather were fastened to an undergarment. Fishscale armour, often associated with the Vikings,was certainly still worn in this period, perhaps by those who could not afford mail, or who found its weight irksome. Odo is shown wearing a different form of body armour to the rest, some sort of tunic made up of black and red triangles over his mailshirt. This presumably indicates his special rank both as a bishop and the Duke's half-brother, and perhaps also his non-combatant status. On the Tapestry, he is shown, like the Duke, not fighting but issuing orders, brandishing his mace of office like a field marshal's baton.

Helmets

The similarity between Saxon and Norman body armour as shown on the Bayeux Tapestry, extended to helmet design. Both sides wear a conical helm with a prominent nasal guard of the kind made famous by films and television. The Tapestry shows porters carrying helmets using these nasal guards as handles, together with the 'mail coats' suspended on a pole - perhaps the first coat hanger in history. 1066 helmets have a conical or slightly convex profile, and were worn over a hood of chainmail, which was evidently not fastened to it but laced under the chin instead. Unfortunately no helmets from this period have survived. They were evidently made of one or more pieces of sheet iron, reinforced by rivetted metal bands around the rim, and from end to end. Cheaper ones may have been made from boiled leather, with or without iron fittings. Eleventh century helmets were like crash helmets, good enough to save the wearer from a glancing blow or a spent arrow, but not enough to ward off a direct hit from a sword or an axe. Some helmets may have been gilded or

Different styles of helmet in use in the eleventh century. Note how even a simple nasal guard 'dehumanises' the man into a warrior. The Viking Society

decorated, though those on the Tapestry look like 'standard issue'. Such a one from the century before Hastings, found at Coppergate in York is highly ornamental, with side-pieces and a curtain or aventail of mail attached to the brim. Its edge-bindings are of brass, the ridge-bindings and nasal of copper alloy. This fancy helmet might have been used ceremoniously rather than as combat headgear. A different kind of helmet was worn by some of the Norman archers, and is known as a kern's hat. It was probably made of formed or boiled leather, and had a characteristic forward-flopping peak. It seems a precarious kind of headgear, but was presumably better than nothing. Archers were not expected to square up to axe-wielding housecarls.

Spears

Spears were the standard infantry weapons of 1066, a cheap, all-purpose weapon adapted for defence or offence. On the Bayeux Tapestry there is hardly a scene without a few spear-carriers, some of them idly leaning on their weapons, others carrying a spear across the shoulder, like a musket. The Tapestry designers represent them as a line of thread, sometimes with a nasty-looking blade at one end, sometimes with a flimsy barb, like a matchstick arrow. In real life, they would have been more substantial. A typical infantry spear was seven or eight feet long, with an ashwood shaft, and a long socketed blade, with a couple of prongs to prevent it getting stuck in one's opponent. Some may have been boar spears, drafted into military use. Spearheads found by archaeologists are rarely barbed. Some have long, angular heads, designed to pierce chainmail. Others have broad, leaf-shaped blades. The cavalry lance was normally held overarm to thrust at the enemy, rather than couched under the shoulder as in later centuries. In only one case is a knight shown charging with a couched lance. Perhaps the ground was too steep and rough at Hastings to charge home in the classic way. The spear's main drawback was a tendency to shatter. According to his chaplain, Duke William was found with the stump of a broken lance in his hand. Javelins were used by infantry, and in great quantity on either side at Hastings. On the Tapestry, a number are travelling both ways during the opening stages of the battle.

Banners

Hastings was a colourful battle. Banners and pennants fluttered above the massed infantry, and on the lances of the knights. Several types of banners are shown on the Tapestry. The commonest, flown by both sides, is a small square pennant with a dagged trailing edge. Another type is half-moon shaped, with a tasselated edge. These bore recognisable patterns and colours, and no doubt had the same purpose as later standards and flags - to fly the regimental colours and form a rallying point in battle. Count Eustace carries what was probably the Papal banner, a white standard with a gold cross. In addition, the Normans flew a barbaric raven banner, perhaps similar to the 'Landwaster' banner of Harald Hardrada and inherited from William's Viking ancestors. A triangular, tasselated standard of this type appears on a coin minted in York the previous century, during the transient reign of the Viking Sihtric Sihtricsson. Years later it was believed that William the Conqueror bore a blue banner decorated with gold lions. This was probably a later invention, but it is quite likely that the Duke did bear a distinctive personal banner as well as the Papal one, just as his father, Duke Robert, had borne a distinctive gold banner while on Crusade.

The dagged, stiff-looking pennants of the English army were probably of traditional design. A similar square war-banner appears on English coins three centuries earlier. In addition, we know that at Hastings, King Harold flew two special standards. His personal one was 'the Fighting Man', a figure of a warrior

Norman standard-bearers wearing the characteristic conical helmet of the age, with its nasal piece and carrying differently shaped tasselled pennants.

picked out in gold threads and precious stones, some say based on the naked giant at Cerne Abbas in Dorset. The other was the Dragon of Wessex, designed like a windsock to inflate in the breeze and give the appearance of flying. It was no doubt more impressive in life than the feeble, weasel-like thing shown on the Tapestry.

Maces

A mace is an upmarket club, used to bash in the head of one's opponent. Maces of later centuries were made of iron, with knobbed, flanged or spiked heads. They were usually carried by cavalrymen, since the weapon was too short to be of much use to a foot soldier. The use of maces at Hastings is interesting and unexpected. They seem to have been primitive, home-made weapons - 'stones hafted onto wooden handles' in William of Poitiers' phrase. Some were designed for throwing - like stick grenades without the bang. There is one in mid-flight on the opening scenes of the battle on the Bayeux Tapestry. Longer wooden maces are carried by Duke William and Bishop Odo, probably not as weapons but as batons *(baculum)* of office. This is an early example of the symbolic use of the mace, later taken on for the office of the sergeant-at-arms, and later still for the authority of Parliament.

Some of the fyrd were armed with maces, according to the Tapestry. Some are still carrying them as they flee from the field. These have knobbly heads, and were presumably studded with iron nails or studs to make them more effective. All the same, if

Fyrd men carrying maces as they flee the battlefield.

all these men had to defend themselves was a wooden mace, it is surprising they didn't run away sooner!

Bows and arrows

Duke William had plenty of archers in his army, King Harold relatively few. Probably most of Harold's archers had been left behind by the rapid march from Stamford Bridge. Possibly, then as later, the best bowmen came from distant counties, like Cheshire or the Welsh marches, which, having troubles of their own, were poorly represented at Hastings. We know that Harold had archers at Stamford Bridge, as did Ealdorman Bryhtnoth at Maldon where 'bows were busy'. The solitary English archer shown on the Bayeux Tapestry would in more normal circumstances have been in good company - despite Henry of Huntingdon's assertion that the English came to Hastings 'without even a quiverful of arrows'.

There are few surviving bows of this period from England, but several found in an eighth century grave in Germany were surprisingly large - up to seven feet long, and made of yew: full-scale longbows in fact. Those on the Bayeux Tapestry seem smaller, perhaps nearer four or five feet long. They may seem small only because, belonging to a lower caste, the tapestry makers routinely designed their archers as dwarfs, and furthermore banished most of them to the margins. Although archers helped the Duke to win at Hastings, they were not as effective as English and Welsh longbowmen would come to be. The problem was not so much bow design as poor technique, for the practice of

Norman archers, two wearing leather 'kern hats', a third, perhaps the commanding officer, in mail and holding arrows in his left hand for rapid fire.

drawing the bowstring to the jaw or chest rather than the ear reduced their range and accuracy. The lethal range in 1066 was only about fifty yards compared with a couple of hundred in the heyday of the longbow. A further drawback is that special military arrows were not used at this date. Eleventh century arrows, called 'billets' by the English, were adequate for bringing down deer and game, but were less effective against armoured troops. They were more deadly when fired high to land on upturned faces - as King Harold was to find out. In Beowulf this sort of experience is termed the 'iron-shower'. What did the archers do when they had run out of arrows? Probably they scavenged the field for spent arrows. The supply of these would have increased as the enemy was pushed back. All bowmen carried a leather quiver, shaped like a duffel bag on their belt or shoulder, which was set upright on the ground beside him when shooting. One archer has drawn all the arrows from his quiver and holds them in his left hand for rapid firing. Most archers at Hastings wore close-fitting cloth tunics and a characteristic leather hat, which suggests some sort of uniform. Only one archer is shown in mail and a helmet, and only one, near the end, is mounted.

Duke William also had crossbowmen. They are mentioned by William of Poitiers, and the *Carmen* refers to their characteristic four-sided bolts, adding that shields were no protection against them. Crossbows at this date were probably simple weapons, drawn by hand. Unfortunately none are shown on the Bayeux Tapestry. They had greater range, penetrative power and accuracy than longbows, but were more slow to load.

51

Axes

The double-handed axe was a weapon the housecarl made his own. Originally a Viking weapon, it had been adopted by professional English warriors and by 1066 had become a battle-winning weapon. The secret of the axe was a long cutting edge of about ten inches, made of specially hardened steel which transmitted the maximum force with the minimum effort. Some preserved Viking axe-heads have an extended blade - the so-called 'bearded' axe, to assist a downward chop, but those at Hastings are shown with a simple

An eleventh century flared axe-head, the chosen weapon of the English Elite.

curved blade flaring trumpet-like from the shaft. The axe-head was attached by its socket to a light ashwood haft about three feet long. The Tapestry shows some longer hafts as tall as a man, but, since none are shown in use in the battle scenes, their use may have been largely ceremonial. Axes could be swung over the head downwards or sideways in a slashing movement, or twirled in a figure-of-eight rhythm, the haft rotating lightly in the hand. The great axe was a powerful weapon, capable of killing a horse and cutting through the mail of its rider. Apart from demanding a tall, strong man to wield it effectively, its main weakness may have been a propensity to snap at the head. The Tapestry shows one such incident, and captures the hapless look of the disarmed housecarl, moments before he is struck down. Another scene suggests that axemen may have fought in teams, with a shield-bearer to protect his master as he fought, and a third man standing by with a lance.

Smaller axes, of the sort used to trim wood and top branches, were used as missiles. On the Tapestry, one man in the close-packed English shieldwall is holding a small axe overhead, evidently in the act of hurling it. As with the flying mace, it suggests desperation.

Cavalry

Mounted 'knights' (*milites*) formed the elite of Duke William's army. William used their speed and mobility to surround and eliminate portions of the English fyrd, and eventually to break up the shield-wall. The Normans and their Gallic neighbours lived much of their lives on horseback, whether travelling, hunting or on campaign. Judging from the Tapestry, Norman horses were small, sturdy beasts, of no more than fourteen hands, with arched necks like chess knights, and notably small heads. The Tapestry shows them, rather obviously, as stallions; some indeed seem to be in a state of sexual arousal. Stallions have the naturally aggressive temperament required of a warhorse. Their equally natural skittishness was controlled by a vicious curb bit, which locked the animal in a vice, forcing it to stop, as well as prick spurs to encourage it to gallop. Except at the charge, the horses were ridden on a tight rein. William himself sat on a black Spanish charger, a gift from King Alfonso of Aragon (on the Tapestry, it changes from black to brown and back).

The riders sat on a high war-saddle, protected with a tall pommel rolled forward at the front, and an equally tall, hip-hugging cantel in the rear. The saddle was held in position by a shock-absorbing breast band as well as saddle-girths. The stirrups were held on long leather straps reaching half way to the ground. The knight rode with a straight leg, as though standing

Mounted Norman knight equipped with spear and kite shield.
Illustration by Jon Wilkinson

upright. A firm saddle and long stirrup straps gave him a firm platform for delivering a blow or a spear-thrust at tremendous force. Cavalry were the shock troops of eleventh century army and were very effective against poorly trained infantry. To counter them, Harold depended not on his own cavalry, as in other European armies, but, like his kinsmen in Denmark, on the powerful counter-stroke of the axe.

With the exception of a mounted archer, all of William's knights wear mail or fishscale hauberks and conical helmets with prominent nasal guards. They ride gripping the reins with their shield arm, and with a spear or sword in the other. Most bear a kite-shaped shield, protecting the whole of that side of the body. The light cavalry spear was normally used as a lance or a javelin rather than the couched spear of medieval romance. The cavalry at Hastings probably did not try to charge straight into the English ranks, but reined in and turned the horse on its heels at the last minute, allowing the rider to strike his target from several feet away. Only at a later stage, when the English were much weakened, did they manage to smash their way through with swords. William's cavalry were apparently organised in small units of eight or a dozen men under a leader carrying a pennant on his lance. The loss of horses at Hastings probably exceeded their riders. William is said to have three horses killed from beneath him, and the Bayeux Tapestry has some striking images of mounts tumbling head over heels or swivelling away from a descending axe.

An eleventh-century foot soldier's marching kit, including wooden bowl, spoon and knapsack as well as sword, shield, harness and helmet.
The Viking Society

Chapter 4

1066: MILITARY ORGANISATION

The English military system

The English army of 1066 was made up of professional soldiers or housecarls (*huscarl*), along with levies from the shires led by their local thegn and known as the fyrd. The image of the English housecarl is of a big, moustached man, clad in mail with a conical helmet and a kite-shaped shield, swinging his heavy, two-handed war-axe. Housecarls were men of privileged status, attached to the household of the king or an earl as paid bodyguards and companions - the name means simply 'household man'. Unfortunately little is known about the housecarls of 1066, or how many of them there were. We know the names of only a few of them - Tostig's men, Amund and Ravenswort, who were killed in the uprising of 1065, and, among Harold's affinity, Scalpi, Gauti and Tofi. Interestingly, these are all Danish names, though their owners probably did not consider themselves Danish. The housecarls of an earlier generation were elite Danish troops used by King Canute to keep the English in their place and enforce the king's will. One of their jobs was collecting taxes, as two housecarls were doing when they were set upon and lynched by the irate citizens of Worcester in 1041. King Harold's housecarls were of a later generation, more integrated into the social fabric, with estates of their own, and a sense of belonging to the English landowning aristocracy, a kind of officer class. Scalpi, for example, had been presented with the estate of Leighs, in Essex. Some housecarls served on garrisons in the boroughs, keeping the king's peace and the fortifications in good repair. Others would have been household men, escorts of the king and his earls, familiars of the mead-hall and the court. They were trained in the martial acts, skilled at fighting with lance, axe and sword. They rode to battle, but fought on foot. The Tapestry shows them lining the front ranks of the shield-wall, dependable troops, sworn to defend their lord with their lives. With a life of honour and privilege came an acceptance of danger and death.

The men of the fyrd performed military service in return for their land. They were 'national servicemen', not a standing army, more of a volunteer fire-brigade, called out only in emergencies.

But they were not an ill-disciplined mob of down-and-outs. Service in the fyrd was linked to the agricultural economy. Each county was meant to levy one man for every five hides of land, a hide being a farmed holding based not on acreage but on economic value (so a hide on poor land was much larger than one on fertile ground). Berkshire, for example, could furnish 500 fyrdmen, and England as a whole about 14,000. This represents about one man for every twelve families, or one per seventy to a hundred inhabitants. The fyrdman was an indentured soldier, paid and equipped not by the state but by his own community. Those identified in the Domesday Book as having fallen at Hastings are described as 'liberi homines'; freemen. We also have William of Malmesbury's comment that most of Harold's army were 'stipendiaries', that is, paid soldiers, together with 'mercenaries' (perhaps his interpretation of housecarls), plus a few soldiers 'from the provinces'. The fyrdman, then, was not a landless peasant but a freeholder, someone with land and property to defend and so with a stake in the outcome.

In 1008, the king had ordered that every eight hides of land must provide a helmet and a mailcoat. Whether this order still applied in 1066 is unknown, but if not, the same principle would have applied, that is to ensure that men presenting themselves for military service were properly equipped. In close combat with edged weapons, a man without a helmet or body armour was not going to last very long. The weapon he carried was perhaps his own choice. Only the better trained would have been skilled with the axe or sword, and many fyrd men from the provinces probably carried a simple spear forged by the local blacksmith. But survival for anyone enlisted to fight at Stamford Bridge or Hastings would depend on the best equipment the man could possibly afford.

There were two kinds of servicemen in the fyrd. The natural leaders were the thegns and prelates (Hastings had an interesting assortment of prelates and clergy on both sides). These men answered the king's summons, delivered by the royal reeve. The rest were drawn from the lower rungs of free society, men who held land under local lords, and who answered their summons. Hence the king would summon a local lord, and it was his duty, at pain of the forfeiture of his lands, to ensure that he called up the due complement of men, in good order and properly equipped. The customs of Berkshire, recorded in the Domesday Book, enact that a man was paid four shillings per hide for his contracted two months of service. It was rare for service to be extended, except under direst emergency - as it was in 1066.

The fyrd was summoned by county shire-reeves or sherrifs. It was unusual for the whole kingdom to be mobilised. Between 1046 and 1065 the national fyrd was called up only three times - in 1051, 1052 and 1065, each time to counter rebellion and prevent civil war from breaking out (which was done by denying troops to the rebels as much as by any particular military activity). But the national fyrd had not been involved in actual warfare since 1016. Harold's Welsh campaigns used relatively small, mobile and well-trained forces, drawn locally and from the professional elite. A large ill-trained army was an impediment to manoeuvre and awkward to supply for long periods. Fyrd service did not necessarily involve fighting. The exact nature of service varied from one place to the next. Local summonses might be made for fortress repair (*'burhbot')*, that is stockades, walls and ditches, or bridge repairs (*'brycgeweorc'*), or for garrison duty in towns. Coastal towns supplied men for ship building or repair. The coastal towns of Kent and Sussex mustered crews of *lithsmen* (sailors) for fifteen days service, once a year. There was also a levy in which each region or 'ship-soke' was to supply and maintain a sea-going ship.

Documents tell us something about eleventh century military organisation, but little about the quality of the troops. How good a fighter was the fyrdman of Hastings? Probably a freeman would have some knowledge of arms - and the right to carry them - and could ride a horse. The upper-classes - thegns and magnates - would certainly have been expert horsemen. As Frank Barlow remarks, 'no man of that rank walked any distance'. William of Poitiers related an occasion when, because of the steepness of the slope, Duke William dismounted and walked. So uncharacteristic was it that Poitiers thought the story would amuse his readers. The ordinary fyrdman may have served his lord more than once against robbers or pirates, and acquired some experience of campaigns, especially if he lived in the usual trouble-spots - the marches of Wales, the Atlantic coast, the Channel towns, or in the unruly north. But there had not been much opportunity, at least in recent years, for battle training.

The fyrdman of 1066 probably fought alongside men from his own burgh or county under the local thegn. Used to an outdoor working life, he could endure long marches and bad weather.

Some, at least, would have brought a horse or pony. It seems that each fyrd man brought his own rations of preserved food - grain, onions, leeks, cheese, perhaps salted meat, supplied by the community and enough for two months service. On the other hand, the images of the Bayeux Tapestry suggest a wide gulf between the well-equipped warrior-class and the rest. Some of Harold's fyrd lack even a helmet, and seem to have arrived at the battlefield dressed for a day's ploughing. Was this just the tapestry designer's fancy? Or perhaps these poorly armed men were not the fyrd at all, but locals, men with burnt cottages and roofless families to avenge, who turned up on the day of the battle?

The Norman military system

Eleventh century Normandy was a dangerous place. William, its Duke, went to war practically every year between 1047 and 1060. The impression of Norman history is of a continual swirl of limited war, revolving around mobile raids and sieges of static positions, especially castles. For the warrior-class it was a way of life, possibly quite a pleasurable one. For those at the receiving end, it must have been a struggle for survival, with fire and sword piled on top of the everyday problems of famine, poverty and disease.

A Saxon housecarl armed with sword and axe.
The Viking Society

The Normans are popularly regarded as the introducers of the feudal system - 'the Norman yolk' - to England. Scholars now debate the extent to which mid-eleventh century Normandy was a feudal state. The concept of a tenancy - land for rent - was changing to one of fiefs, in which homage and fealty was performed in return for grants of land. The terms included military service of up to forty days, similar in practice to the English fyrd. Such service did not

The men of Dinan in Brittany defending a wooden castle against the Normans. The English do not seem to have had castles, relying instead on walled towns.

apparently extend to foreign wars, and William's invasion army contained what were in effect professional soldiers, either in the service of the Duke or one of his lords, or mercenaries from surrounding lands willing to work on credit terms. Every great lord had his own retinue of soldiers, who lived at his hall at his expense, or were settled on holdings on one of his estates.

At the core of William's army were his own affinity of knights, men whose fortunes he had built up and who rewarded his generosity and success with their loyalty. Among them were the Duke's half-brothers, Robert Count of Mortain and Bishop Odo of Bayeux, together with boon companions like William fitzOsbern, Walter Giffard and Roger of Montgomery. It was their wealth that paid for the more expensive items in William's invasion plan, like ships and war-horses. The military life created close companionships and a sense of *esprit de corps*. For William's Normans, success fed national pride which spilled over into arrogance. The Norman Conquest was so brutal and thorough because the English were regarded by them as inferiors, socially, militarily and culturally.

A Norman foot-soldier in a mail hauberk with strips of metal reinforcing the forearms.
The Viking Society

The Norman way of making war was based on mobility - squadrons of mounted 'knights' (*milites*) - and static defences, that is, castles. To take territory you had to capture castles, and this was done either by threats, siege or direct assault. Most Norman castles were a collection of wooden buildings surrounded by a palisade, which in turn stood on an artificial mound. They were nearer in concept to hill forts than the stone castles of later times. A stubbornly defended castle could be starved out by ravaging the surrounding land, but the ravagers were in turn vulnerable to attack by a relief force who often operated by ambush. William was renowned for turning the tables on his enemies in this way. This kind of warfare, and its interaction with different continental neighbours, created a military professionalism still alien to the English. The speed in which William could load and unload an invasion force which included prefabricated castles, wagons and tools, horses and their gear, and all kinds of provisions and supplies is still impressive. He must have had good junior officers and NCOs, as well as men that took a pride in their work. Equally, the Duke obviously had personal qualities that created confidence on his own side and fear in the enemy camp. William's Normans were on a steep learning curve - while the English relied on the ancient customs of war.

Chapter 5

YORK AND STAMFORD BRIDGE

Harold and Tostig: the star-crossed brothers

Tostig (also spelt 'Tosti') was the third son of Earl Godwin, and for ten years he had ruled the Anglo-Danish earldom of Northumbria. As an outsider in a turbulent area, he probably had the hardest task of all the Godwin brothers. Yet his rule seems to have been tactless, and was marked by long absences. It all came to a violent end in October 1065, when, while Tostig was away at court, a group of Northumbrian thegns entered York with their supporters and slaughtered 200 of Tostig's tenants and officials. They seized and carried off his treasure and effects, declaring Tostig an outlaw and replacing him as earl with the young Morcar (or Morkere), brother of Edwin, earl of Mercia. Evidently Tostig had made himself unpopular by levying a heavy tax. According to John of Worcester, the trigger for the revolt was the assassination of the popular Northumbrian thegn, Gospatric, apparently with the connivance of the queen. Behind it lay long simmering resentment to rule without consent. Tostig was the king's favourite. The rebellion threatened to turn into a civil war between old King Edward (who never visited northern England) and the northern rebels. The king, and Tostig, were ready for war. The king's chief negotiator, Harold, was not. He advised that the north would not accept Tostig back at any price, and that the king should accept their terms and send his brother into exile. Tostig saw it differently: probably always jealous of his brother, he now accused him of complicity in the rebellion. Indeed, he even suspected Harold of being behind it.

More likely, Harold was reluctantly recognising a *fait accompli*. However the actions of Tostig in 1066 make sense only if we assume the displaced earl was convinced of his brother's treachery, and was determined to bring him down and restore his own fortunes by fair means or foul. Tostig sailed with his family and a band of faithful retainers to the court of his brother-in-law, Count Baldwin of Flanders. He may have visited Duke William in Normandy. In May 1066 he appeared off the south coast with a fleet of sixty ships, and ravaged coastal settlements (perhaps those belonging to his brother) from the Isle of Wight to Thanet.

He was seen off, but Tostig headed north, ravaging as he went, to the Humber and his former earldom. There, in a stiff engagement with a land army under Edwin and Morcar, Tostig had the worst of it. Some of his men deserted, and Tostig continued on his way with a reduced fleet of twelve ships. Eventually he took refuge in Scotland, where he was welcomed by King Malcolm Canmore, the 'Malcolm' of Shakespeare's play, *Macbeth*.

Tostig's raids were pin-pricks of no great military significance, but they had a disproportionate effect on Harold's strategic dilemma in 1066 in that they obliged Harold to call out the fyrd earlier than he might have wished. Harold's first concern was to keep the south coast in a state of readiness to oppose the expected Norman invasion (see chapter 6). If Tostig could sail, so could William. For all Harold knew, Tostig might have been the advance guard of a full invasion. Harold sailed from Westminster to Sandwich and waited there for his household troops to gather. He is said to have assembled naval and land forces larger than any in living memory. Along the south and east coast, local militia, under their respective thegns, mustered at their assembly points. prepared for a possible invasion. They must have had some form of signalling system, perhaps a chain of beacons, though no chronicler bothers to describe it. Church bell towers, like that at Bosham, doubled as look outs. In May, Harold's ships sailed from Sandwich to the Isle of Wight, which the king made his headquarters for the whole of the summer of 1066. Why Harold chose the Isle of Wight for his base is a mystery. It might have

English warships preparing to anchor with the aid of plumb-lines and sounding-poles. The Bayeux Tapestry shows English ships larger than the Norman ones, with elaborately carved prows and sterns.

formed a good lookout station in clear weather, but the summer of 1066 was damp and overcast. He might have wanted to be upwind of any Norman crossing, but Harold would not have had time to manoeuvre his fleet to intercept, nor would the realities of medieval boat construction allow fleet action to take place on the high seas. In the end, his most likely reason for being there

A modern reconstruction of a Viking landing party.

was to guard the natural harbours of the Solent and the road to Winchester. But as the 'C' Chronicle relates, in despair, 'it was all to no purpose'. As so often in 1066, Harold's strategy is hard to understand. However, his thinking may not have been entirely defensive. According to the 'E' Chronicle, at some time during the summer, an English fleet sailed 'against William', presumably in a raid on the Norman coast. It may have been led by an Ethelric or Ailric, who the Domesday Book mentions as partaking in a naval battle against William and falling ill on his return. Unfortunately nothing more is known about the outcome.

The normal period of fyrd service was two months. This expired at the end of June, but Harold kept them out until September. Keeping the 'national service' in readiness, and presumably well-supplied, for more than four months was a military achievement unparalleled since the days of Alfred. Possibly he had organised things so that the fyrd operated its coastwatch in relays. Even so, by 8 September, Harold had run out of provisions, and the fyrd was forced to disband. July was the month when fresh food was scarcest, while from August the men were needed for the harvest, invasion or no invasion. This was the essential weakness of the English system: the harvest created a gaping hole in Harold's defensive plans, whilst it favoured the enemy who could strike England's villages and farms while at their most vulnerable, and live off the land in the process. Traditionally the sailing season ended in mid-September, before gales made Channel sailing too dangerous. Harold must have hoped the crisis had passed for that year. He himself sailed to London, not without loss, arriving in the capital, feeling far from well, on 20 September. In the meantime, 200 miles further north Harald Hardrada had arrived. The crisis had, in fact, just started.

Some time during summer, Tostig, brooding at the failure of his personal invasion plan, decided to go for broke and throw in his lot with the Vikings. He set sail for the court of the king of Norway, Harald Hardrada, and, according to the 'D' Chronicle, offered his allegiance and 'became his man'. There is no record of diplomacy between England and Norway over the disputed succession, and the ensuing invasion seems to have taken Harold by surprise. Probably Harald Hardrada, who was, for once in his life, not at war with anybody, simply took advantage of an open invitation to invade the north of England while Harold was busy in the south. Tostig was a useful figurehead, a potential puppet ruler in the north. Tostig himself seems to have imagined that he still had friends in England, though, as events were to show, he had none.

Most of what we know about Harald's and Tostig's invasion comes from the great *Heimskringla* saga by Snorri Sturluson, written down more than a 100 years after the event. According to him, Harald 'sent word throughout Norway, raising a half-levy of the whole army'. The summons caused much excitement, some reckoning that nothing was too difficult for Harald Hardrada, while others thought England was too populous to conquer easily, and that her housecarls were worth two Vikings. The army assembled in the Solund Isles, near Trondheim. It was said that King Harald had over 200 warships, as well as supply-ships and smaller craft. Some estimates put it at much higher: Geoffrey Gaimar, writing in about 1130, says Harold and Tostig together led 460 ships.

In Harald Hardrada's own words:

> In the mists
> Of the moonless bay
> Our dragon ships
> Lurk at anchor
> Awaiting the dawn.

Yet, according to Snorri, there were portents of coming disaster. Men dreamed of an ogress riding a wolf, rending and devouring the flesh of fallen warriors. Harald himself was warned in a dream by his dead brother Olaf that death awaited him in England, and that wolves would tear his body. The fleet set sail during the summer, most of the ships landing at Orkney where they were joined by local Vikings under their local jarls (earls) Paul and

Erland, sons of Thorfinn. Moving south on the same northern wind that was keeping William in port, he arrived at the mouth of the Tyne to rendezvous with Tostig and his much smaller fleet. Their ships now descended on the unprotected coast of Yorkshire with sword and fire. They destroyed the town of Scarborough by building an enormous bonfire on the cliffs and pitchforking the burning embers onto the thatched roofs beneath. From Scarborough they ravaged Holderness, brushing aside a local resistance, and, rounding Spurn Point, passed into the Humber. Harald's objective was York, one of the largest towns in England, and the administrative centre of the north.

Harald Hardrada decided to march against York rather than risk his ships beyond the influence of the tide. He moored his fleet on the River Ouse, ten miles from the city, at Riccall, probably pulling the ships onto the shore using wooden rollers rather than anchoring them by the bank. The English had been given enough advance warning of Harald's invasion to raise a sizeable army to defend the town. Very probably, the fyrd of Edwin and Morcar and their thegns were on standby that summer, just as Harold's men were in the south. Scarborough and other towns had been left undefended so that the young earls could concentrate their force at York. There they decided to offer battle.

The Battle of Fulford

Gate Fulford was the first and least known of the three great battles fought during the fateful autumn of 1066. It resulted from the decision of the northern earls, the brothers Edwin and Morcar, to engage the Norsemen in battle before the arrival of

Fulford Battlefield on a bright spring morning, still marshy today. The broad River Ouse is in the background.

King Harold with the larger forces of Wessex and East Anglia. In hindsight, at least, it was a battle that need not, and probably should not, have been fought. It is nonetheless important in our story because defeat at Fulford destroyed the army of the northern earls, and prevented their participation at the Battle of Hastings. In that sense, it contributed to the Norman victory. Why was it fought at all? The best guess is that power play was involved. Edwin and Morcar were attempting to defeat the invaders and the hated Tostig by their own efforts, and thereby reassert their political independence. Despite their alliance, sealed by Harold's marriage to their sister, Aldgyth, they may have distrusted Harold, suspecting that he might make a deal with his brother Tostig by restoring him to the earldom of Northumbria at the expense of Morcar. They clearly considered themselves strong enough to beat the invaders on their own. There may have been other factors - the harvest, perhaps an inability to feed the army for more than a few weeks - that we know nothing about. For whatever reasons, all the leading players in 1066 worked towards bringing matters to an early conclusion by a decisive battle.

The only detailed source for the Battle of Fulford is *King Harald's Saga* by Snorri Sturluson (see p33). Although it is in error in at least one particular - in prematurely killing off Morcar - we are lost without it. King Harald Hardrada's objective was to seize York, the effective capital of northern England and one where Scandinavians and English had long lived together in harmony. From this base in the north, he may have hoped to conquer the rest of England bit by bit, as he had done in Norway, and as a Viking predecessor, Sweyn, had done in England in 1014. The probability that Tostig would rule in northern England as a subking gave a personal dimension to the forthcoming battle. Tostig and Morcar, both younger sons of the two greatest houses in England, were mortal enemies.

Having moored his ships on the riverbank at Riccall, some nine miles (fourteen km) from the city, Harald and Tostig marched on the city through flat, marshy country, probably along the Roman road now followed by the A19 between Selby and York. At Gate Fulford, by the bank of the River Ouse, two miles from the city walls, Harald's scouts sighted the English host filing out from York and taking up positions athwart the Viking's line of advance, between the river and the village of Fulford. Clearly a battle was in the offing.

We know very little about the army of Edwin and Morcar. The Saga insists it was 'an immense army'. The *Anglo-Saxon Chronicle*, probably more accurately, says it was 'as great a force as they could get'. But the combined force of Edwin and Morcar could well have numbered 5,000 fighting men. York alone, with over 1,500 households, could muster about 1,000 men, and anticipating the invasion, the brothers could have called out men from the Midlands and Northumbria as far as the Scottish border. According to Geoffrey Gaimar, the army was mustered from seven shires (by implication, Yorkshire, Lincolnshire, Cheshire, Nottinghamshire, Derbyshire, Staffordshire and Lancashire, as Durham, Northumberland and Cumbria were not then considered as shire counties). The core of the army would have been formed from the housecarls of the two earls, joined by the levies of the shires under their respective thegns or sherrifs. Though the earls had been given at most three to four weeks warning of Harald Hardrada's arrival, the army they raised was as large as any seen in England since the Danish invasions half a century earlier. Earl Edwin's force was probably mustered at his administrative capital at Chester, and may have included Welshmen, who had a recent history of alliance with the house of Leofric. If so, they faced a 125-mile forced march to York, and may have arrived only a few days before the battle. Morcar would have mustered his own thegns and household men at York. Gathering a force competent to take on a full-scale Viking invasion in a matter of weeks is another sign of the efficiency of Saxon mobilisation.

The parish of Fulford, on the east bank of the Ouse, south of York, used to be divided into two: Water Fulford and Gate Fulford. 'Gate' is from an old word meaning road: Gate Fulford means 'the road through the foul (i.e. muddy) ford'. The best clue to where the battle was fought is supplied by *King Harald's Saga*, which places the standard of the Norse King near the river, among the thickest press of spears, with the rest of his army stretching inland towards a dyke 'where there was a deep and wide swamp, full of water' - presumably the 'foul ford'. The only site that matches this description is the Germany Beck which enters the Ouse from its headwaters in the present-day campus of the University of York. Although now straightened, and most of its marshes long since drained, the beck surely marks the

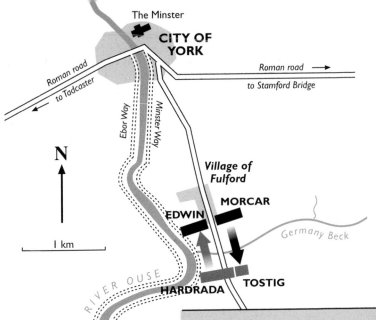

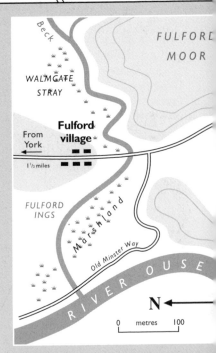

approximate centre of the battlefield. Edwin and Morcar used the stream to strengthen their front, while the gap between the river and marshland near the village gave them a natural defensive 'choke point'. But the Norseman, too, were in a strong position. Just south of the stream there is rising ground which the Norsemen occupied. They too had the stream to their front, and the river to their flank, but they too had the opportunity of turning the Saxon position using the 'dead ground' behind slightly rising ground to the east.

The Battle of Fulford was fought on 20 September 1066, 'on Wednesday, being the vigil of the feast day of St

The Battle of Fulford as interpreted by Charles Jones of the Fulford Battle Group. (See www.battleoffulford.org.uk

Matthew the apostle'. It was mid-day or early afternoon. The army of the English earls approached the Norsemen in close formation, a moving wall of shields. Morcar, leading the vanguard, faced Tostig on the Norwegian right flank, with Edwin's Mercians facing Harald Hardrada nearer the river. In the clash of the spears around the ford, Tostig's division was pressed back. According to the chronicler of Worcester, the English 'fought so bravely at the onset that many of the enemy were overthrown'. But after a long contest, the English buckled under Norwegian counter-attacks, and fled with great loss. Snorri Sturluson, of course, ascribes the Norwegian victory to the personal valour of Harald Hardrada. Noting that the English were heavily engaged on Morcar's flank, the Norwegian king decided on a decisive counterthrust. With a war-blast of horns or trumpets, Harald personally led a fierce onslaught onto the English right. The fighting was intense but

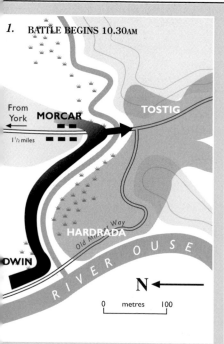

1. **BATTLE BEGINS 10.30AM**

1. At first light the Housecarls of Edwin and Morcar move along the Germany Beck to block the road to York. Later they are joined by the earls leading the fyrd to reinforce the flanks. The Viking host arrives at about 10am. Morcar attacks at the ford with initial success. Along the Beck the English successfully fend off Viking attacks.

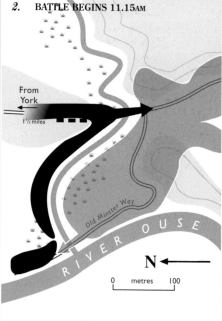

2. **BATTLE BEGINS 11.15AM**

2. Viking reinforcements arrive. With the two sides locked together along the Beck, Harold Hardrada leads a devastating charge along the riverbank against earl Edwin. Edwin's housecarls die where they stand but the levies break up and flee back to York.

brief. Outfought, the English broke into flight, 'some fleeing up the river, and others down the river ... many were lost in the water; the drowned sank to the bottom'. While Harald's son, Olaf, pursued the English to the gates of York, the Norsemen rolled up the English flank, thereby trapping many of Morcar's men in the swamp. King Harald himself composed a haku-like poem on their fate:

> (Morcar's) warriors
> All lay fallen
> In the swampy water,
> Gashed by weapons;
> And the hardy
> Men of Norway
> Could cross the marsh
> On a causeway of corpses.

Fulford was a marshy battle, fought in shallow water and mud.

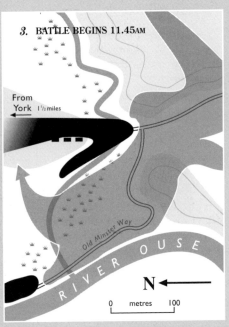

3. Harald Hardrada, having beaten Edwin, rolls up the north bank of the Beck to attack Morcar in the flank. Seeing the Vikings coming up behind them, many of Morcar's levies flee.

4. The Viking right swings across higher ground to descend on Morcar's other flank. The remaining English lose the bank and concentrate around the road and village, are in danger of encirclement. Edwin and Morcar retreat to York bringing some order to the beaten English. York is safe for the moment.

According to Florence of Worcester, more were drowned in the river than slain in the field. The 'causeway of corpses', though probably a clichè, was the one thing people remembered about it long afterwards. The English account, in the *Anglo-Saxon Chronicle*, is brief. Both sides suffered significant losses ('great slaughter'). Many English were slain or drowned, or put to flight, and the Norsemen had possession of the field. Both earls survived, however, and escaped behind the walls of York with at least part of their army. Though the Vikings apparently believed him to be slain, Morcar lived to fight another day. In fact, he was a professional survivor, the one great Englishman of 1066 to survive all the troubles and die in his bed.

The maps on pages 69 - 71 show the progress of the Battle of Fulford as interpreted by the local Battlefield Trust Group. It assumes that the Vikings outnumbered the English (which I regard as questionable), and were able to envelop and crush the

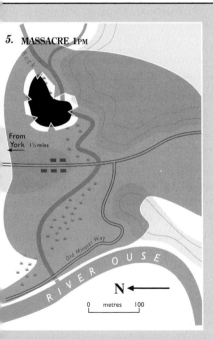

5. A force of perhaps 500 English try to fight their way out through the morass, but are massacred. Fighting continues along the river and at Heslington, a mile to the west of Fulford but Harald Hardrada has already won a victory. York surrenders on terms two days later.

Germany Beck, now a field drain, with Fulford village on higher ground above the river terrace. Here Harald Hardrada led his successful charge against Edwin's Mercians.

71

Fulford village on river terrace

MORCAR

HARDRADA

River flood plain

River flood plain

The flood plain at Fulford with the modern village on higher ground to the east. Harald Hardrada began to roll up the English flank.

defenders of York as reinforcements arrived and with the help of a ridge of 'dead ground' to disguise Harald's outflanking manoevre. During the 1990s, skeletons in what appears to have been an ancient cemetery were uncovered during riverside development at Fishergate in York where once stood the church of St Andrew, the nearest to the battlefield of Fulford. Carbon-dating of a sample of bones indicates that half of the remains are from a single violent event in the mid-eleventh century. Although there were several large-scale battles and uprisings at York before and after the Conquest, there is a strong chance that these are the bones of men from the army of Edwin and Morcar that fell at Fulford. Some showed serious injuries that show no signs of healing, and so were probably the cause of death. They include sword cuts to arm and leg bones, cracked or decapitated skulls, and point injuries caused by spear thrusts or arrows. At least one was covered in multiple deep cuts, as though the corpse had been hacked and stabbed. There are more than twice as many injuries to the left hand side of the body than to the right, which suggests that these were soldiers using a similar technique of fighting. There are also many injuries to the back, suggesting that some

The River Ouse near York, where many men drowned trying to escape from the carnage at Fulford. Note the steep river banks.

victims were finished off after they were knocked to the ground. The many cuts to the thigh bones suggest a favourite stroke of the Vikings, perhaps against a man on horseback, or to bring an opponent down by slashing his unprotected legs below his shield. A find like this brings an ancient battle to life. From a dry sentence or two in a chronicle, we are suddenly confronted with real people who faced the edged weapons of the invader perhaps with nothing more to protect them than faith and a leather tunic.

Harold: from London to York

Only five days separate the Battles of Fulford and Stamford Bridge. For Harald Hardrada they were busy days. The city of York surrendered on terms. Tostig, as the Saga reminds us, knew everyone in town. Among the 150 hostages taken from York were sons of all the leading men. According to the *Anglo-Saxon* ('C') *Chronicle*, the city 'also helped with provisions', which has been interpreted as evidence of a willingness by the people of the north to submit to, and even aid, the Norwegians. However, others fled to join King Harold. On 24 September, Harald Hardrada moved part of his army eight miles east of the city to Stamford Bridge to await the arrival of further hostages from the shire.

Why Stamford Bridge? Probably because this small settlement by the River Derwent lay on a crossroads, equidistant between York and the Norse fleet, still moored at Riccall. The army could be supplied from there by boats. Moreover, Stamford Bridge stood on the boundary of the North and East Ridings, and between the wapentakes (administrative districts) of Picklington, Acklam and Bulmer. Hence, Harald probably chose the place for political as well as logistical reasons. He was certainly not expecting to have to fight a battle there. It is evident he had no idea that King Harold's army was fast approaching. On the day of the battle, a warm, dry day in early autumn, the Norsemen had stripped to their shirts. Many had left their mail and heavy gear behind with the ships.

News of the Norwegian invasion probably reached Harold around mid-September, perhaps as he arrived in London having disbanded his army. At once, the king set about raising a new force large enough to take on the Vikings. How he managed to do so in so short a time is one of the mysteries of 1066. From the Domesday Book there is evidence that men joined him from as far and wide as the estate of Witton in Worcestershire, from

Paglesham in Essex and possibly Ramsey Abbey in Cambridgeshire. The 'C' Chronicle states that Harold marched north by night and day, as quickly as he could 'assemble his levies'. His way north followed the Great North Road, Ermine Street, a straight Roman road whose surface and many bridges must have been kept in good repair. Harold and his household must have been mounted to reach York in so short a time - perhaps nine days at twenty-five miles per day. However, assuming Harold set out on around 16 September, that would not have allowed time to collect any forces other than those he still had with him. Levies from the shires probably joined him at prearranged muster points along the way, for example at the burghs of Huntingdon, Stamford and Lincoln. During the journey, Harold learned of the disaster at Fulford, knowing now that he would have to face the Norwegians without much help from Edwin and Morcar. Undaunted, he carried on, intent on reaching York as soon as possible to prevent the Norwegians from consolidating their hold on the north. He was also counting on taking the enemy by surprise. It was a bold strategy, which risked tiring out his men. Alfred Burne, the doyen of battlefield studies, considered the Stamford Bridge campaign 'a feat of endurance that it is hard to match, far less to beat'. It was a tribute to the organisational and logistical strength of the English army under King Harold.

King Harold marshalled his forces at Tadcaster on the River Wharfe, perhaps expecting an attack from York, and where he may have rendezvoused with English ships, bottled up on the River Ouse. Survivors from the Battle of Fulford joined him with news that the Norsemen were camped at Stamford Bridge

The River Wharfe at Tadcaster. Harold's army crossed the river by ford at this point. The old Roman road they took is still visible as a depression on the opposite bank.

unaware of the danger. With his usual boldness, what the 'D' Chronicle calls at this point 'our king Harold' decided to attack at once. At dawn on Monday, 25 September, the English army crossed the Wharfe along the Roman road called the Ebor Way, and reached York a few hours later. After the briefest pause for rest and reinforcements, he set out again towards Stamford Bridge.

The Battle of Stamford Bridge

It could hardly have been earlier than noon on that clear, warm day that Norwegian scouts spotted a cloud of dust from the east, from the neighbourhood of Gate Helmsley. Straining their eyes, they glimpsed the silver twinkle of mail coats and shield bosses glinting in the sun. King Harald asked Tostig who they could be, perhaps some of his kinsmen seeking his protection in exchange for their fealty? As they waited, the cloud grew closer, and, in a vivid memory set down years afterwards, saw 'glittering weapons sparkled like a field of broken ice'.

Now realising what was upon them, and taken completely by surprise, Harald dispatched three of his strongest riders to Riccall with urgent orders for the ship-men to come on, fully armed, with all speed. In the meantime he needed to get those of his men camped on the west bank of the Derwent across the river to join his main force, now forming up on the rising ground east of Stamford Bridge. The river is too deep to ford here and was crossed, then as now, by a single bridge, probably of timber resting on stone piles. It would not, however, have been a narrow footbridge, as in some reconstructions. It carried a main road, linking York with the rich land of the East Riding. By eleventh century reckoning, it was a big bridge. An advance picket of Norwegians formed a defensive line in front of the bridge, while detachments filed across to the far bank. Inside the line, Harald Hardrada, clad in a blue tunic, wearing an elaborate helmet, and riding a shiny black horse, encouraged his men. At one point, according to the Saga, the horse stumbled, pitching the king forward over its neck. Unhurt, he sprang to his feet, crying 'A fall is fortune on the way'. This may be an echo of a similar yarn told of Duke William at Hastings.

King Harold of England rode forward with twenty of his housecarls, all clad in mail. He had a message for his brother, Tostig. He offered him peace, and with it Tostig's former earldom

The fruitless parley just before the battle at Stamford Bridge. Harold pictured left, is conversing with his brother Tostig, Harald Hardrada is on the far right of the picture.

of Northumbria. More than that, Harold was prepared to give him a third of all England to rule over. Tostig is supposed to have answered as follows:

'This is very different from the hostility and humiliation (you) offered me last winter. If this offer had been made then, many a man who is now dead would still be alive, and England would be in a better state. But if I accept this offer now, what will you offer King Harald Sigurdsson for all his effort?'

Then came the famous answer:

'Seven feet of ground, or as much more as he is taller than other men.'

Tostig told his brother to make ready for battle. He would not now desert the King of Norway, and, at his side, he would conquer or die. The parley over, Harald Hardrada, who either did not understand English or was out of hearing, asked the name of the man who had spoken with Tostig. On being told, he remarked that though lacking in inches (at least compared with Harald), the man stood proudly in his stirrups. But had he learned in time that it was none other than Harold Godwinson, he would have had him slain on the spot.

The Norsemen having made a successful fighting retreat across the bridge, only one man, a mail-clad, axe-wielding giant,

was left, straddling the wooden planks like the hero Horatio, in *Livy's History of Rome*. He is supposed to have successfully defended the bridge against all comers, even evading an arrow shot at him, and was overcome only by a devious stratagem. While the giant swung his axe, someone slipped under the bridge in a swill tub, thrust his spear through the planks beneath the giant's outspread legs, and transfixed him (*þurustang* = 'through-pierced')

in the nethers. Down fell the warrior, as Harold's men raced across. This story is told by the English in a late addition to the Chronicle, made perhaps 150 years afterwards, and is not mentioned in the Saga. It may be based on a real event, but as told it is probably a yarn. Harold had archers and slingers with him, and it would have been foolhardy to allow a celebrity-seeking Viking to buy time for the Norwegian army. Fact or fiction, it is the best remembered event of the Battle of Stamford Bridge. In the nineteenth century, the village used to hold a dinner on the anniversary of the battle, featuring a dish called 'swill-tub pie'.

The real battle took place on the rising ground east of the present-day village, long known as Battle Flats. The site is crossed by a Roman road, now the A166, and another ancient track, known as Minster Way, which linked Stamford Bridge with Beverley. Then, as now, the battlefield was farmland, probably a mixture of stubble fields and pasture with the deep Derwent winding past. As at Fulford, only *King Harald's Saga* gives details of the battle. According to Snorri, Harald Hardrada drew up his army in a long

Harold's view of Stamford Bridge and the River Derwent from the Roman road at Gate Helmsley. Then, as now, the land was probably open fields, cultivated as strips.

The modern Stamford Bridge, built downstream of the original bridge in the 1730s. A strong current flows here and there are no nearby fords. The only way across the Derwent was the bridge.

thin line, with the wings bent back until they met. The king stood inside the circle of spears under his raven banner, the Land-Waster, carried by a man named Fridrek. With him were his best men and his archers. Tostig stood slightly apart, with his own bodyguard and banner. The short speech put into Harald's mouth by Snorri is in heroic vein:

'We never kneel in battle before the storm of weapons, and crouch behind our shields. Rather, I will carry my head high to the heart of the foe where swords seek to shatter the skulls of doomed warriors. If I die, my sons will avenge me. God's will be done'.

Nevertheless, it was the English that attacked. We can only imagine them, housecarls manning the front line, advancing behind a wall of kite-shields, spears held shoulder high, their eyes glittering between helmet and shield. Both sides fought on foot. Snorri is almost certainly in error in describing repeated charges by mounted Englishmen. There is no other warrant that the Anglo-Saxons fought in this way. By the time he was writing, memories of Stamford Bridge had become muddled up with Hastings. The *Carmen* of Hastings, composed much nearer to the

time, says rather that the English 'scorn the solace of horses, and trusting in their strength they stand fast on foot'. E.A. Freeman, the Victorian historian of the Norman Conquest, went so far as to call Stamford Bridge the last English battle fought in the ancient manner, 'shield-wall to shield-wall, sword to sword or axe to axe'. King Harald Hardrada

78

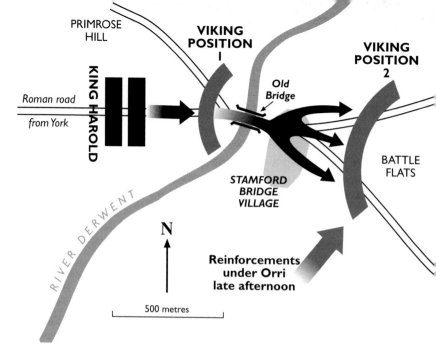

PRIMROSE HILL

VIKING POSITION I

Old Bridge

VIKING POSITION 2

KING HAROLD

Roman road from York

STAMFORD BRIDGE VILLAGE

BATTLE FLATS

N

Reinforcements under Orri late afternoon

RIVER DERWENT

500 metres

seems to have attempted to repeat his success at Fulford, putting himself at the head of a dramatic countercharge. This time it didn't work. Snorri's dramatic account of the death of Harald Hardrada, slain early on in the battle by an arrow through the throat, is probably true. A more satisfying ending would have had him die at the end of the battle, perhaps in a climactic duel with King Harold. With the great Norwegian king having choked to death on his own blood, there was a lull in the fighting, during

The aftermath of the battle at Stamford Bridge. Harald Hardrada lies dead with an arrow in his throat, whilst Harold (far right), mourns over the corpse of his dead brother, Tostig.

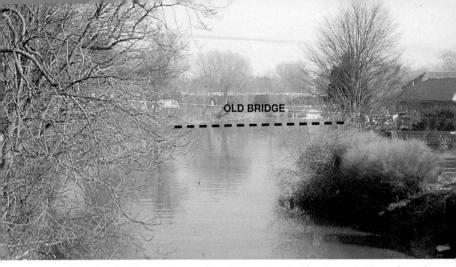

OLD BRIDGE

The river looking upstream from the modern bridge towards the weir and site of the old bridge.

which the English king again offered quarter. At this point, late in the afternoon, Norse reinforcements led by Eystein Orri arrived from Riccall, dusty and blown from running in their heavy mail coats. Hence, the final phase of the battle was known as 'Orri's storm'. Refusing quarter, the Norsemen fought on with despairing fury, some of them casting off their mail, others collapsing unwounded from exhaustion. The English pushed through to the raven banner where Tostig was cut down. The *Carmen* asserts that Harold himself, like 'another Cain', fought his brother, cut off his head, and buried head and trunk in the ground. However, since the same author has William personally killing Harold at Hastings - and brother Gyrth, too, for good measure - it is more likely he thought it poetically appropriate. Orri, too, fought to the death.

In the words of the Norse poet Arnor:

> It was an evil moment
> When Norway's king lay fallen;
> Gold-inlaid weapons
> Brought death to Norway's leader.
>
> All King Harald's warriors
> Preferred to die beside him,
> Sharing their brave king's fate,
> Rather than beg for mercy.

80

A Viking noble wearing a cloak over his mail byrnie, outside his wooden thatched hall. The Viking Society

Only Styrkar, Harald Hardrada's marshal, found a horse and got away, shivering in his bare shirt. He later waylaid a carter and killed him for his fur-lined leather coat. By sunset, the host of 'Norwegians and Flemings' were dead or in flight. There is no mention of prisoners in any of the sources, and this was an invading force that had twice refused quarter. They could expect no mercy. There were no kinfolk to bring home the bodies. According to Orderic Vitalis, writing seventy years later, the battlefield was still strewn with human bones. Of the English casualties we know nothing. They must have been substantial, but the only known victim is an unnamed thegn of Worcestershire, an uncle of Abbot Aethelwig of Evesham. Indeed, we know the names of very few of Harold's men at Stamford Bridge. According to a late, untrustworthy source his brother Gyrth, at least, was with him, and perhaps Leofwine too. Other leading men may have included Edwin and Morcar, Earl Waltheof, Marleswein, sheriff of Lincoln, and Oswulf of Bernicia. But the English had no Snorri to sing their praises in lamplit halls, long afterwards. The nearest they had was this downbeat lament from Goscelin, a monk of St Bertin, probably written after the Battle of Hastings. As a patron of Queen Edith, Goscelin was mourning for Tostig; for them both, victory was bitter-sweet.

And who will write that Humber, vast and swoll'n
With raging seas, where namesake kings had fought,
Has dyed the ocean waves for miles around
With viking gore, while heaven mourns the crime?

Harald Hardrada's view across the Derwent from the Roman Road (now A166) near Dane's Well on the Battle Flats above the present day village.

> What madman writes of this, at which the mind
> Grows faint and ears are shocked? Report feels shame
> At such a crime. For whom shall I write now?
> This murderous page will hardly please the queen
> Their sister........

Late in the day the English pursued the beaten remnants of the Norse army to their ships at Riccall. There, according to the *Anglo-Saxon Chronicle*, there was more fighting, and many more Norsemen fell:

> 'Some were drowned, others burnt to death [in the ships?] and thus perished in various ways, so that there were few survivors, and the English had possession of the place of slaughter.'

There is archaeological confirmation of these events in the form of human remains uncovered in fields around Riccall over the past 150 years. So far some sixty skeletons have been unearthed, some showing apparent battle wounds. Bob Stoddard, a pathologist commissioned by the BBC for the historical series, *Blood of the Vikings*, found telltale signs of war in a slashed arm bone and a pierced

The now featureless battle flats looking north from Minster Way (Moor Road). In this vicinity the Viking 'Landwaster' raven banner flew at Stamford Bridge.

The Battle Flats looking south towards High Catton. Many eyes looked this way during the battle for signs of the long-awaited reinforcements from the ships moored at Riccall.

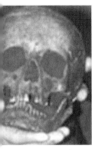

An unearthed skull of a Viking killed in the conflict. Many of the bones had tell tale signs of a violent death.

sacrum, evidently the result of a spear thrust to the lower body. Back at the lab, a new forensic technique was used to establish which part of Europe the bodies came from. Because tooth enamel is formed in childhood and remains unchanged throughout an adult's life, it can yield clues about a person's homeland. Trapped in the enamel are oxygen isotopes (molecules of different atomic weight) whose composition varies from country to country. The consistent pattern revealed by these 1,000-year-old teeth shows that their owners were not English but Scandinavian. Almost certainly they were raiders, and since they date from around the mid-eleventh century, there is a good chance that they are none other than Harald Hardrada's men, cut down in the last struggle around the ships. Further tests may prove or disprove this diagnosis. If correct, they are mute witnesses of the Battle of Stamford Bridge. Not so much as a bone has been found on the main battlefield; the piles of whitened bones mentioned by the twelfth century historian have long since weathered into dust. (There are reports of unusually small horseshoes found on the field.)

The Minster Way follows an ancient track across the Battle Flats present in 1066.

Stamford Bridge was not only perhaps the greatest victory of Englishmen against Vikings, it marked the effective end of the Viking age.

Harald Hardrada's army was wiped out. With nowhere to run, the Viking losses at Stamford Bridge may have been proportionately greater than that of the English at Hastings. Perhaps 4,000 bodies lay in the fields and marshes between Stamford Bridge and Riccall. Harald's sons, Olaf and Magnus (whom the *Anglo-Saxon 'C' Chronicle* calls 'Hetmundus'), and Tostig's, Skuli and Ketil, were spared, perhaps on the grounds that they had not been present at Stamford Bridge. So, for the same reason, was the young Jarl Paul of Orkney. After swearing oaths of peace and friendship, they were allowed to depart. But only twenty-four ships out of the original fleet of 300 returned to Norway, implying that only about 500 to 1,000 men survived the battle. The other ships were either requisitioned by Harold, along with a great treasure, or burned. Nothing is known of the fate of the hostages from York. One hopes it was kinder than that of Canute's, taken under similar circumstances half a century earlier, left behind on the beach minus their hands, feet and noses. The bodies of Hardrada and Tostig were treated honourably. The latter,

identified from a wart between the shoulders, was interred in York Minster, while the king was eventually returned for burial among his ancestors in Norway.

Why did the English win so decisively at Stamford Bridge? Most eleventh century battles were won by attrition rather than Napoleonic stratagems. Once battle was joined, a leader's ability to command and control was limited. His main task was to set an example. In terms of quality, the sides were well-matched. Harold's men, in particular, must have been superbly fit and well-motivated to have endured so long a march, followed by a hard-fought battle with heavy axes and swords. They had the crucial advantage of surprise, catching the Norsemen on a hot day at the riverbank, in many cases minus their mail shirts and so vulnerable to blows from edged weapons. Although we are, as usual, in the dark about numbers, it is possible, indeed likely, that the English army was larger. Assuming the Norse ships carried twenty-five men on average, Hardrada would have a total of 7,500

A local artist's interpretation of the Battle of Stamford Bridge, superimposed on a map of the village.

when they landed at Riccall, of which perhaps two-thirds could have been present at Stamford Bridge. But some Viking ships rescued from the depths by archaeologists are big enough for 100 men. England could, in theory at least, field an army of well over 10,000. John of Worcester says that Harold led 'many thousand well-armed fighting men'. His army combined the remnants of Edwin's and Morcar's with thegns and fyrdmen from his brother Gyrth's populous earldom of East Anglia and Harold's own heartland in the south. It therefore contained detachments from all the earldoms of England. Some sources add that Harold had with him mercenaries from Denmark. It is probable, therefore, that the Norsemen were outnumbered, possibly by as much as two to one.

Finally, Harald Hardrada fatally divided his force, leaving part of it at Riccall with the ships. Given the circumstances, the English should have won the battle. King Harold's victory was due to his ability to bring a superior force to the battlefield and take the enemy by surprise. It was made possible by the high state of alertness of the Anglo-Saxon state, and its efficient system of mobilisation and supply. The Stamford Bridge campaign was a triumph of military logistics as much as might.

Chapter 6

HASTINGS: PREPARATIONS

Duke William and the Channel crossing

There is a story that Duke William heard the news of Harold's coronation on 6 January 1066, as he was setting out for a hunting trip in his forest near Rouen. The Duke reacted angrily, lacing and unlacing his cloak, but spoke to nobody, and nobody dared speak to him. He returned to the great hall of his palace and sat alone on a bench, his cloak cast over his face.

His first reaction was to send emissaries to Harold. In an aggrieved but not unfriendly tone he required Harold to relinquish the crown in conformity with his solemn oath. Harold's reply was to the effect that an oath taken under duress had no force. A second exchange of views was less friendly, and equally fruitless. William prepared for war. A crucial aspect of his diplomacy was to secure papal support. Although the details are not known, William was evidently able to present himself as an earnest ally of the church in contrast to Harold, who, as well as being an oath-breaker, was associated with black-sheep prelates like Stigand. The pope, Alexander II, publicly proclaimed his support for William's enterprise, and presented him with a special banner. Evidently no plea was heard from Harold's side. Papal support was crucial because it turned what might have been more aggression into something of a crusade. It was the eleventh century equivalent of a UN resolution.

The duke exploited his advantage by sending emissaries to the courts of Europe, securing positive noises from Emperor Henry IV and, if the pro-Norman sources are to be believed, even friendly nods from the anglophile Swegn of Denmark and Baldwin of Flanders. More importantly, it enabled William to appeal with confidence for volunteers outside Normandy. As David Douglas put it, 'a crude promise of plunder was buttressed by higher considerations of moral right'. Soldiers of fortune flocked to his banner not only from neighbouring statelets like Brittany and Ponthieu, but from as far away as Aquitaine and Sicily (see page 110). Most, but by no means all, of the leading Normans were willing, indeed eager, to support William with men, money and ships. They were investing in the most potentially profitable enterprise of the century. A list, probably dating from shortly after 1066, records the 'quotas' of various leading Normans for ships and men towards the expedition. Walter Giffard, for example, whose lands included the port of Dieppe, was to provide thirty ships and 100 'knights' (i.e. men with mounts). Hugh of Montfort owed fifty ships and sixty knights, and Odo, the wealthy Bishop of Bayeux, no fewer than 100 ships (which is not to say that all these ships were actually loaned or built). Clearly the expedition was a major undertaking for such men, but the war effort must have involved all levels of society, shipwrights, ostlers, carriers, carters and provenders of every description.

To take enough men, horses and materials across the seas to defeat Harold and put William on the throne was a daunting logistical exercise requiring an enormous transport fleet. The lowest estimates on its size are around 700 vessels (Robert Wace says he had got the seemingly exact figure of 696 ships from his father). The ship list implies 782 full-sized vessels, which, with smaller craft, could take the total to 1,000. William of Jumiéges, writing soon after 1066, says 3,000, Gaimer of Lincoln (who probably didn't have a clue) 11,000. The Bayeux Tapestry makes it clear that some of the ships were scratch-built from green timber, implying that supplies of seasoned timber at the ports had been used up. The scenes of woodmen, shipwrights and carters toiling away with axes, bills, and adzes certainly creates the

William's shipwrights at work, converting Norman forests to clinker-built ships' hulls.

impression of a busy summer in Normandy, but it can only suggest the likely scale of the enterprise. To face the Channel seas, William's ships were designed for sailing, not rowing. They would have been broad in the beam and relatively deep in draft, especially the horse transports, which had to be fitted with flooring for the stalls and ramps. They probably resembled the Viking Gokstad ship, which was twenty-three metres (seventy-nine feet) long and over five metres in beam with a draft of two metres. G.M. Gillmor (1996) calculated that to build just one such vessel would require 128 planks from sixty-four selected, straight-grown oaks. With additional timber for the mast and other fittings, the total, assuming the most economical use of each tree, would be around seventy-four trees. For 700 ships of mixed sizes, this would amount to nearly 52,000 trees, enough to strip large parts of Normandy of its best timber. Furthermore, the timbers would have to be transported by ox-carts to the nearest suitable river or estuary, and then floated to the construction site.

A modern day replica of the square-rigged Gokstad ship, a Viking craft similar to those used by William.

Skilled shipwrights, working in teams of up to twelve, could finish a Gokstad-style craft in about three months, that is, about 1,000 average work days per ship. In the meantime they would need to be fed, as would all the other woodmen, carters, sailors and miscellaneous workers engaged on William's enterprise. In practice, it would probably have been impossible to build a scratch fleet of 700 ships without effectively bankrupting the country. No doubt William and his nobles preferred to beg, borrow or threaten wherever possible, and scratch-build only as a last resort.

The muster area for William's fleet was the mouth of the river Dives, near Dives-sur-Mer, now a silted-up level but then a deep harbour easily capable of holding 700 ships. By August, the army was camping nearby in a large enclosure. With the soldiers were a horde of servants, cooks, armourers and butchers, along with stores sufficient to feed perhaps 10,000 men and 3,000 horses for a month without pillaging the surrounding land. Again, the logistics look remarkable: to maintain 3,000 horses in peak condition for the battle ahead would need about thirteen tons of grain and the same amount of hay every day, on top of the vast tonnage of food, wine and firewood needed by the army. Bernard Bachrach (1996) calculated that a month in camp would consume the equivalent of 9,000 cartloads of food and fuel. Moreover 5,000 cartloads of manure would be going in the opposite direction: William's horses would have produced roughly 700,000 gallons of urine and 5,000,000 imperial pounds of manure in a month! We should also note that the weather that August was unseasonal: of 'foul weather and ceaseless rain', according to the *Carmen*. We do not know how men lived on campaign in 1066. Probably houses were 'requisitioned' wherever possible, but thousands of men must have become used to camping under the cloudy sky in 1066, under cloaks and blankets, perhaps under improvised tents of hides and branches.

William needed all of the month he had allowed for while waiting for a favourable wind. By early September he must have been growing desperate, especially when a gale swept up the Channel on 12 September. William decided to move the fleet to St Valèry in the neighbouring statelet of Ponthieu, much closer to the English coast. The voyage of 100 miles took two days, during which several ships ran onto rocks in a storm. Probably the horses were taken there by the overland route and were spared the journey.

William of Poitiers preserved for us a picture of Duke William looking anxiously at the weather-vane on the church tower at St Valèry forever pointing east as westerly winds swept up the Channel. Suddenly, after offering prayers to the local saint, Valeria, for a favourable wind, the weather changed. 28 September was a hot, sunny day with a southern breeze. After morning mass and a devotional procession of the relics of the saint around the camp, the army embarked. If they were not on board already, the horses were now coaxed onto the ramps with up to ten animals per transport. The Tapestry has them peeping over the side, but more probably they were tethered in covered stalls. At high tide, at around three in the afternoon, the ships were rowed out of

William's fleet crosses the Channel on a fair wind. The horse transports are shown as larger than the troopships.

harbour to an assembly point just off the coast, in water shallow enough to anchor in. Each ship carried a lantern in the masthead for the night journey. William's own ship, the *Mora*, a gift from his wife Matilda, led the fleet. There is a fine picture of it on the Tapestry, its figurehead a carved lion, and on the stern post a boy holding a banner and blowing an ivory horn. The men laid their shields along the gunwhales, Viking fashion, as protection from the spray.

The ships set sail in formation, perhaps in staggered lines. Aiming to arrive at the natural harbour of Pevensey just after daybreak, they needed their lanterns, for it was a moonless night. After all the anguish and toil of the previous six weeks, the actual crossing seems to have been uneventful. With a following wind, the fleet moved sedately at an average speed of five knots. The Duke's faster ship raced ahead of the fleet at one point, but by

*William's ship, the **Mora** with a square rigged sail and lantern perched high on the mast.*

early morning the long shingle beach at Pevensey Bay came in sight. The only mishap was a small group of ships that became detached from the main fleet and landed further down the coast at Romney, where some of the Normans were killed when attacked by the local fyrd.

Harold: Stamford Bridge to Hastings

The Battle of Stamford Bridge was fought on 25 September. Two days later the wind changed, allowing the Normans to cross the Channel and land at Pevensey on the morning of 28 September. Messengers carrying the news of William's landing and Harold's victory rode flat out in opposite directions. Harold could not have heard of the landing much sooner than the start of October. A Victorian print preserves the moment, with Harold's

A messenger interrupts the banquet given by Harold with the news of the Norman invasion.

housecarls slumped at the mead-bench as the king reacts at the alarming news. Harold was busy with the aftermath of a hard-won victory, tending the wounded and resting his weary and depleted forces. He now had to find yet another army to fight William. The fyrd that served at Stamford Bridge were in no state to march again. One source says that some northerners refused to serve Harold further since he had refused to share out the loot from Stamford Bridge as was the custom. Another claims that Harold replaced the unreliable Morcar as earl with Marleswein, the sherrif of Lincolnshire. This is unlikely, since Morcar was still at least the nominal Earl of Northumbria in 1067, when he accompanied William to Normandy as a prize hostage. Marleswein was probably some sort of deputy or minder. Possibly his orders were to raise another fyrd to reinforce Harold in the south.

The dates between Stamford Bridge and Hastings are uncertain, but as Harold was in London for about a week before marching out to Hastings, he must have made the return journey from York in about a week: that is an average of twenty-seven miles a day. As before, he probably rode with the relatively small mounted core of his army, his faithful housecarls, sending out royal messengers to summon the fyrd of the southern and eastern shires. The week or so he spent in the capital would give time for the fyrd to assemble, at least from the counties close to London. It has been argued that the reason Harold was short of archers at Hastings was that, being on foot, they had been left behind on the road. More likely, the fyrd of Hastings was a completely fresh force, the third or fourth raised that year. There was insufficient time for large forces to march from York to reach Hastings in mid-October. The new army seems to have drawn heavily on the men of Berkshire, Essex and Kent. As with William, the church came to Harold's aid. The *Domesday Book* records tenants of several abbeys fighting for Harold, including Bury St Edmunds, Abingdon, St Benet of Holme and St Augustine's of Canterbury, as well as Harold's uncle, Abbot Aelfwig of the New Minster in Winchester. He was joined in London by his brothers Gyrth and Leofwine with their forces. Together, the *Anglo-Saxon Chronicle* tells us, they formed 'a great host'.

In his march from York to London, Harold was in great need of haste. He needed to be in the capital to organise England's defences and deal with William. But the speed in which he pushed on to the attack attracted criticism, then and now. (For example, the *Abingdon Chronicle* blames him for placing too much confidence in his own strength, and advancing with less than proper caution.) Most sources agree that his intention was to catch the Normans unaware, to surprise the enemy with boldness and speed, as he had done at Stamford Bridge. But unlike Harald Hardrada, Duke William was expecting, indeed inviting, an attack. Harold's strategy at Hastings is hard to understand, but he must have had powerful reasons to seek an early conclusion. Perhaps the most likely explanation is that he intended to bottle William up near Hastings by positioning his army across the narrow neck of land eight miles from that town where the London road ran across a ridge between tidal marshes. This would prevent William from laying waste the hinterland of Sussex and force him to attack Harold on the ground of his own choosing. Possibly Harold was even intending to attack William, once his army had been fully assembled. I discuss this aspect of Harold's strategy more fully in chapter 10. Harold's plan was to muster his army at 'the hoar apple tree' on Caldbec Hill, some eight miles inland from Hastings and so within striking distance of William's army. 'Hoar' (grey)

The windmill (now a private residence) near the summit of Caldbec Hill, the site of the 'hoar apple tree'.

probably meant the tree was covered with lichens, signifying that it grew in the open, and was probably old and gnarled. The hoar apple tree was evidently a well-known landmark, probably a large crab-apple, of the sort often mentioned in Anglo-Saxon charters. Presumably men from Kent, Sussex and perhaps Wessex were expected to join Harold there by prearrangement. At the same time, Harold also sent orders for his fleet of perhaps seventy ships to set sail as soon as the wind was favourable to prevent William's escape by sea.

While Harold was in London, William sent an emissary to parley with him. According to Robert Wace, his name was Hughon Maigrot (Hugh Margot), a monk from

Fècamp. The justice of William's claim was repeated, and then, in the Norman version of events, William offered to submit his case to either French or English law, and, furthermore, to save lives, challenged Harold to a duel. Harold's response was to place the ultimate judgement in God's hands, and to announce that he would march at once to give battle (if so, so much for taking the enemy by surprise!). David Crouch (2002) has argued that the subtleties of French diplomacy went right over the solid English heads. The purpose of the parley was not, of course, to secure a truce but to wrong-foot Harold by making him seem unsure of the rightness of his claim to the throne.

The distance from London to Senlac Ridge is fifty-eight miles, much of it on tracks through forest in hilly terrain. Harold's average of nineteen miles a day was less than he achieved three weeks before, but still remarkable for a force of perhaps 6,000 or 7,000 men, strung out on narrow, muddy tracks, many of them marching on foot. Leaving London on 11 October, he arrived at the hoar apple tree just before nightfall on Friday 13 October. Legend has it they spent the night drinking and carousing. In fact, as General Fuller put it, 'Harold's men were dog-tired and slept like logs'.

William: Pevensey to Hastings

In 1066, Pevensey was a small coastal community based on fishing and salt manufacture. Its great days were long behind it, but standing proud on a rib of land surrounded on three sides by water was a reminder of past glories - the shell of the old Roman Channel fort, Anderida. The coastline was very different from now. Then a lagoon with its associated creeks and salt pans penetrated far inland over the area now known as Pevensey

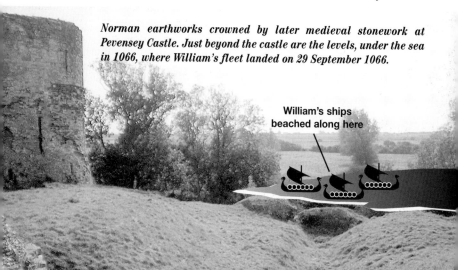

Norman earthworks crowned by later medieval stonework at Pevensey Castle. Just beyond the castle are the levels, under the sea in 1066, where William's fleet landed on 29 September 1066.

William's ships beached along here

Levels. Long since drained, it is now farmland grazed by cattle or under crops. The site of the Norman landing now lies a mile inland. In 1066, Pevensey lay within a natural harbour protected from the seas by a shingle bar with a broad entrance roughly where Pevensey Bay village now stands. The Normans arrived there at low tide. The fleet either negotiated the entrance channel in line or beached on the mud and shingle. One of William's reasons for choosing this landing place was the size of the harbour, large enough for his entire fleet. Another was a readymade castle, which his engineers immediately fortified further with an inner rampart topped by a timber palisade.

The story goes that William missed his footing as he stepped from his ship and fell flat on his face. What might have been construed as a bad omen was turned around by a quick-witted soldier who quipped: 'Thus you hold England in your hands, O future king!' If Robert Wace is right, William had expected resistance and conducted a tactical disembarkation, his archers jumping out first to provide covering fire. But none was needed. They burned and looted Pevensey all the same - twenty years later, the *Domesday Book* describes much of the land hereabouts as still 'waste'.

William was now in a dilemma. While he probably knew that Harold had stood down his army three weeks earlier - for spies were busy in both camps - it is unlikely he had learned of Harold's dash north to counter the invasion of Harald Hardrada. Pevensey offered a good harbour but poor communications. However, a few miles further up the coast lay the port-town of Hastings, also with a suitable harbour and defensible thanks to the narrow neck of land formed by the shallow estuaries of the Brede and the Bulverhythe (now, as at Pevensey, drained farmland). Hence, if things went badly, the Normans could defend their beach head while conducting a fighting retreat to the ships. By digging in at Hastings, William must have expected to fight his battle there. Until the enemy was brought to battle and defeated, it

The modest monument to the Norman landings at the entrance to Pevensey Castle.

was essential that he maintained contact with his fleet. Knowing Harold as he did, the Duke was expecting him to attack. Leaving a garrison at Pevensey, most of William's army, including the mounted cavalry, probably marched to Hastings overland, circumnavigating Pevensey lagoon and reaching the town from the north on 29 September. Favourable winds and tides enabled the fleet to reach the port at about the same time.

Roman stonework at the base of the Saxon shore walls at Pevensey Castle. William's army camped within these walls before moving on the Hastings.

By contrast with Pevensey, Hastings lies on a receding coast, and the site of the Saxon town is now partly underwater in the area of the pier. William built the second of his timber forts on the clifftop above the town where the ruins of Hastings Castle now stand. The grassy mound within the later curtain wall may be the remains of William's motte, shown on the Bayeux Tapestry. While some men dug or hauled timber up from the ships, others foraged in the surrounding countryside. The Tapestry shows them, evidently under the command of one Wadard, requisitioning cattle, sheep and pigs for slaughter. Cooks and serving-men knocked up a feast for William and his nobles, served on shields and eaten on long benches. Odo, prominently, blesses the food - duck or chicken roasted on spits, fish from the market - and wine drunk from bowls.

What else the Normans were doing is displayed on the Tapestry's next scene. It is an icon that stands for the plight of refugees down the ages, as a woman and her child are evicted from their home while two Normans in civilian costume torch the

Interior of Pevensey Castle today. The stonework is medieval, but the green marks the site of the Norman inner fortification of 1066. After the Conquest, this was given to William's half-brother, Robert of Mortain.

roof. There must have been a lot of burning. The taxable value of the villages of Hailsham, Herstmonceux, Ashburnham, Crowhurst, Filsham and Horstede fell by half between 1066 and 1085, when the *Domesday Book* was compiled. Much of the land was still 'waste', twenty years later. Only the manor of Rye was spared, since it had been promised to the Abbey of Fècamp, some of whose monks were present in William's army. Rye in fact, increased in value over the same period from £34 to £50. The purpose of William's ravaging was twofold. It was the quickest and cheapest way of collecting supplies, and it was also likely to enrage King Harold when he heard about it, especially as these were Godwin lands. According to one story, Harold's faithful reeve was hanged slowly from the gable of his own manor house in Crowhurst.

William was in touch with Normans in England. One of them, Robert fitzWimarc, an important court official under Edward the Confessor, sent him word of Harold's great victory at Stamford Bridge. His advice, according to William of Poitiers, was to remain behind their fortifications and avoid battle for the time being, for Harold would surely destroy him. As we might expect, William replied that he had no intention of hiding behind ditches and palisades, and would engage with Harold as soon as possible. It is probably true that William was not thinking defensively. He intended to fight, and needed a battlefield where he could use his cavalry to best advantage. At the same time, he could not risk being separated from his supply lines. What he might have done if Harold had played a waiting game is an interesting question. It was late in the season for Channel sailing, and if he stayed where he was, he would suffer losses from dysentery and other maladies of a large, stationary army. Probably he would have advanced further along the coast, taking Dover and establishing winter quarters thereabouts. The two weeks William spent at Hastings gave him time to scout the surrounding land. He had also sent Hughon Maigrot to King Harold, and no doubt had spies keeping him informed of Harold's movements. Around dusk on 13 October pickets came galloping into camp with the news that Harold's army was near. William took precautions against a night attack, presumably by posting pickets on all routes from Hastings, and ordered his army to stand to arms during the night.

At daybreak (about 5.30) on 14 October, a Saturday, William heard Mass, took communion and hung around his neck the sacred relics on which Harold had sworn his oath. His strategy of sitting tight and provoking an early encounter had been successful, and he must now seize the initiative at once. And so, runs the Bayeux Tapestry in its usual cryptic way, the Normans went out 'TO DO BATTLE AGAINST KING HAROLD'. On the way he met a scout called Vital, who is shown pointing behind him. A little later the Normans reach a hill, probably Telham Hill, a mile from Senlac Ridge where another rider points with his shield towards a wooded ridge. The Tapestry now cuts to the English position where a look out shades his eyes against the low morning sun as he stares south towards Hastings. A comrade, or perhaps the same man, rushes back to warn Harold, who is shown mounted on a black horse in a posture of alarm and agitation.

Today one can walk the six miles (ten km) from the castle ruins at Hastings to the crest of Telham Hill in an hour and a half. The route of the modern A2100 is probably close to the line of William's march, which he seems to have managed with great efficiency, getting his men into position by about eight o' clock. According to the *Anglo-Saxon Chronicle*, William's advance was unexpected, catching the English by surprise 'before all of his host came up' ('E' Chronicle) or 'before [Harold's] army was set in order' ('D' Chronicle). John of Worcester goes further, claiming that less than a third of Harold's army had arrived. Furthermore,

William, holding the Papal banner, receives news of Harold while his men burn the homes of Harold's tenants. The woman and child are perhaps the first pictured refugees in history. Is the bald figure in the centre a portrait?

The fourteenth century Gatehouse to the Abbey grounds, as grand an entrance to a battlefield as any in Europe.

he adds, 'inasmuch as the English were drawn up in a narrow place, many retired from the ranks, and few remained true to him'. Since, as it turned out, Harold's army was at least large enough to fight William almost to a standstill, the chronicler was presumably exaggerating here, perhaps making excuses. But there is a hint of corroboration in the 'D' chronicle when it says that the king fought 'most resolutely with those men who wished to stand by him'. Probably Harold's army had become strung out along the narrow road, where men had camped for the night and had not yet caught up. Perhaps, too, there had been desertions. The news that Duke William was flying the papal banner and that Harold had been condemned as an oath-breaker might have caused faint hearts to think twice. But the narrowness of the ridge at Senlac Hill meant that it would have been difficult to deploy a larger army there. It was probably not numbers that mattered so much as Harold's lack of archers and cavalry, and hence his ability to counter-attack a force with plenty of both. His most serious mistake was in mustering his forces too close to the enemy camp. William was in a hurry. By about eight o' clock, the armies had sighted one another. The Battle of Hastings was about to begin.

Chapter 7

HASTINGS: THE ARMIES

The ridge at Senlac

The Battle of Hastings was fought on a saddle of land formed by Caldbec Hill in the north and Telham Hill in the south, about a mile apart. The site, with its hillside and plain, has often been compared with Waterloo (and, like it, had probably been long earmarked by Harold as a potential battlefield). As defined by English Heritage, it is small and compact, and covers not much more than a square kilometre. Ever since 1070, the ridge where the English stood has been dominated by Battle Abbey. Most of the field on which the Norman army advanced to engage them is now open parkland, that is, grassland with scattered mature trees. The marsh, where some of the cavalry enmired themselves, has become a series of ponds along the course of the Ashen Brook, but the sandy hillock where the fyrd of Harold's right wing took their stand, is still there, crowned with a thicket of gorse. The surrounding land was, and still is, thickly wooded; indeed the 100 square kilometers around Battle are one of the most densely wooded parts of England, with about fifty per cent of the land under trees.

The town of Battle did not exist in 1066: the battle itself was its *raison d'être*. However, this was not a wilderness. The area was settled with scattered small villages, which appear under their Saxon names in the *Domesday Book*. The woods, though extensive, were heavily managed for game, outpasture (especially for pigs) and for timber, and were probably rather open. On the Bayeux Tapestry one of the trees has what look like bands on the trunk, and most of them seem to be pollards, that is, trees cut on a regular cycle at about ten feet high.

What did the battlefield look like in 1066? The *Carmen* of Hastings describes how the English poured out from 'the hiding-places of the woods'. The battlefield itself was 'a hill near the forest and a neighbouring valley' where 'the ground was untilled because of its roughness'. In his deathbed speech as recounted by Orderic Vitalis, William the Conqueror referred to 'the heath of Senlac'. By rough ground and heath we should perhaps imagine rough natural grassland with scattered bushes of gorse.

Geologically, the battlefield and its surroundings lie on the Hastings Beds, formed by layers of sandstone and clay. The landscape is undulating, forming hilltops and ridges, with many small streams that in this area feed into the River Brede. Characteristically, the streams cut through porous sands to form deep ravines, known as gills. There are several of these in the vicinity of the battlefield, one of which was probably the famous 'malfosse'. The most likely candidate is Oakwood Gill, a mile north of Senlac ridge (see below). Ashen Brook, too, was more of an obstacle in 1066, described by one source as a deep ditch, which, as the Tapestry makes clear, also flooded into marshland.

Today the slope of Senlac ridge is modest, only eight degrees in the steepest parts and elsewhere between three and five degrees. However, the ridge is concave in profile, and the uppermost parts may have been steeper before they were levelled

View of the battlefield towards Telham Hill, a mile away. William's army deployed downhill in the left distance and formed into a line in the valley just beyond the first line of trees.

William's army deployed here

NORMANS

BRETONS

Panorama of the battlefield from the valley to the ridge showing the length and incline of the Norman advance. The hilltop, which was levelled in 1070, may have been steeper.

to build the abbey and houses in the town. The ridge is more or less straight, running from west to east for 600 metres, although the eastern side has been obscured by modern buildings. Both flanks were guarded by steep slopes giving the Normans no option other than a frontal assault. Harold's line probably conformed with the ridge, at least initially, rather than being bent back into a horseshoe.

HASTINGS: THE ARMIES

The English army

As they reached the heights of Telham Hill, the Normans watched the English army suddenly appear out of the woods and mass along the ridge facing them, spear points glittering in the morning sun. Some were close enough to see King Harold himself ride up and plant his banner on the highest point, roughly in the centre where Battle Abbey now stands. All the English dismounted to fight, as was the custom. As the author of the *Carmen* put it,

> 'the English scorn the solace of horses, and, trusting in their strength, they stand fast on foot, and count it the highest honour to die in arms that their native soil may not pass under another yoke'.

Terrace looking east, a fine stone pine tree marks the eastern end of the English positions.

Some of the housecarls were seen carefully grooming their hair, which the crewcut Normans mistook for effeminacy. One was supposed to greet death well turned-out, like a bridegroom. No doubt the English also knew that cleanliness helped save wounds from becoming septic. Even minor wounds could result in gangrene and death, as was shown by the demise of William Clito, grandson of the Conqueror, from a spear-cut on the arm, or Richard the Lionheart from an arrow-wound in the shoulder.

Harold's plan seems to have been to hold a strong position where the Norman cavalry would be least effective, and take such opportunities as were offered him. As we have seen, the ridge forms a natural defensive position, and it is mainly on its physical parameters that estimates of the size of Harold's army are based. Initially, at least, men in the front-line stood shoulder to shoulder, foot to foot, to form a wall of shields. So close were they massed that 'the men who were killed could hardly fall to the ground', wrote William of Poitiers. The chronicler Henry of Huntingdon compared the famous wall of shields at Hastings with a castle, which the Normans were besieging. The *Carmen* offers a different metaphor: a wild boar brought to bay by hounds but still dangerous, defending itself with his tusks, and who, with foaming jaws, fears neither dogs nor spears. On the basis of hints in Wace's

The abbey terrace looking east.

chronicle, the Victorian historian E.A. Freeman gave the English a ditch and timber palisade along the front of their position. However, much controversy later, the idea has been dismissed. If there were any such defences they were makeshift ones, but no contemporary account mentions any.

In his classic account of the battle, General Fuller allowed two feet per man for the front line to conform with the width of a shield. This would suggest a front line of about 1,000 men, to which Fuller added between nine and twelve rear ranks to form a mighty phalanx of between 6,300 and 7,500 combatants. Another way of calculating numbers is to look at where Harold's men came from. Although we know the names of only twenty or so Englishmen that fought at Hastings, they are enough to show that the army was drawn up mainly from the south-east and East Anglia, from Berkshire and Hampshire to Norfolk and Suffolk. These counties could raise about 5,900 fighting men. In addition, Harold and his two brothers led their own household men. The best guess of their numbers is based on Tostig's household at York, which numbered 200 housecarls (who were apparently slaughtered to a man in the rising of 1065). Harold's household would have been larger, Gyrth's and Leofwine's probably smaller. Snorri Sturluson believed that a third earl, Waltheof, whom he mistakenly took for another royal brother, was present at Hastings, but this is unlikely for no contemporary source mentions him. Snorri's information was a poem in which Waltheof burned alive 100 Normans in an oakwood. It is probably a folk tale based on the prominence of Earl Waltheof in the resistance to King William after the Conquest. According to William of Poitiers, the English were also aided by Sweyn, the King of Denmark, some of whose fighting men had family ties with England. When Sweyn invaded England in 1069, one of his reasons was said to be revenge for the Danes slaughtered by the Normans at Hastings. Perhaps these were the 'mercenaries' mentioned by William of Malmesbury. It also seems that reinforcements were reaching the battlefield throughout the day. Both sets of estimates, based on the ground and on who was present, converge on the figure of about 7,000 combatants. It may have been more. It was probably not much less. It is only a guess, but 7,000 to 7,500 fighting men has become the concensus among historians.

This was probably a smaller army than the one Harold had led at Stamford Bridge. Many there had been wounded or left behind in the rapid march south. In particular it is assumed that Harold had fatally few archers at Hastings because, being without horses, they were unable to keep up. The generally reliable William of Malmesbury asserts that Harold's army was 'top heavy', composed mostly of 'stipendiaries', that is, of paid troops. Many fyrd men, he says, had deserted Harold because he had not shared out the plunder after Stamford Bridge. Others had stayed at home fearing God's wrath if they aided someone whose cause had been condemned by the Pope. By contrast, the Bayeux Tapestry shows a great many poorly armed 'peasants' in Harold's army. The force certainly filled the Norman scouts with awe as they watched it assemble from their vantage point on Telham Hill. Baudri of Bourgeuil likened the massed English spears to a forest. William of Poitiers compared it with the vast barbarian hordes faced by the ancient Romans, at whose coming whole woods were felled and rivers ceased to flow.

The front line was probably manned mainly by the well-armed housecarls. The household men of 1066 were expected to occupy the places of greatest danger. Throughout Old English literature, kings and war leaders are referred to as protectors, responsible for the well-being of those below them in rank. In that sense, the shield wall at Hastings was a metaphor of Saxon society, at a time when the safety of the realm and the protection of the individual had become one. This is what the Bayeux Tapestry may be showing us in the famous scene, the most vivid in its entire length, of the line of tall men in chain mail, their standard foremost, standing in close formation as they face the charging Norman cavalry. The Englishmen at Hastings would have served under the banner of their lord, whether king, earl or thegn. For example, the men of Middlesex probably served under their sherrif, Esegar or Ansgar, who was also an important court official. The men of Berkshire were with their thegns, who included two tenants of Abingdon Abbey, Godric of Fyfield and Thurkill of Kingston. At least two of the senior clergy were present. Aelfwig, abbot of the New Minster in Winchester, was Harold's uncle. Leofric, abbot of Peterborough, was the cousin of earl Edwin. Their role may not have been confined to prayers. There is a tradition that abbot Aelfwig brought with him twelve monks wearing mail beneath their habits, along with the abbey's formal quota of twenty 'knights'.

We do not know where any of these men stood at Hastings,

apart from King Harold himself, who, as far as we know, never departed from his command post in the centre. No source mentions where his brothers Gyrth and Leofwine were, though it is a matter of some importance to the outcome of the battle. Some have taken William of Poitiers' statement that their bodies were found by the king to suppose that the Godwin brothers stood together under the dragon banner. This is unlikely. The earls had their own responsibilities, and it seems more likely that they led the two wings of the army, respectively at the head of the men of East Anglia and the Home Counties. The Bayeux Tapestry has them fighting and going down together, but this may be the designer's editing of the facts. The Norman sources either did not know or were not interested in the exact formation of Harold's army. To them the English were the *rustica gens*, the barbarians as amorphous as the Gothic hordes of ancient times.

NAMED INDIVIDUALS PRESENT AT THE BATTLE OF HASTINGS

† = Killed in the battle or died of wounds

THE NORMAN ARMY (35)

William, duke of Normandy
Odo (half-brother), bishop of Bayeux
Robert (half-brother), count of Mortain
Eustace, count of Boulogne
Geoffrey, bishop of Coutances
Alan 'the Red' of Brittany
Robert, count of Eu
William fitzOsbern
Aimeri, vicomte of Thouars
Turstin, son of Rollo, standard-bearer
Hugh (Ivo) of Ponthieu
Walter Giffard, and son of same name
Roger of Beaumont
William, son of count of Evreux
Geoffrey, son of count of Mortagne
Humphry of Tilleul
Ralf of Tosny
Hugh of Montfort
Hugh of Grandmesnil
William of Warenne
William Malet

Gulbert of Auffay
† Robert of Vitot
† Engenulf of Laigle
Rodulf (Ralf) de Tancarville
Gerelmus of Panileuse
† Robert fitzErneis
† Roger, son of Turold
† Taillefer
Erchembald
Vital
Wadard
Pons
Hugh of Ivry
Richard fitzGilbert

THE ENGLISH ARMY (20)

† Harold, king of England
† Gyrth (brother), earl of East Anglia
† Leofwine (brother), earl of Kent
? Hakon (nephew), son of Swegn
† Aelfwig (uncle) abbot of Winchester
Leofric, abbot of Peterborough
Aelfwold, abbot
Ansgar the staller, sherriff of Middlesex
† Godric, sheriff of Fyfield, Berkshire
† Thurkill, thegn of Kingston Bagpuize, Berkshire
Eadric, a deacon from East Anglia
Aelfric, thegn from Huntingdonshire
Skalpi, housecarl
Alwi of Thetford
Ringolf of Oby
† Breme, freeman
† 'Son of Helloc'
Also two unnamed freemen from Tytherley in Hampshire, and a
'tenant from St Edmundsbury' (Bury St Edmunds, Suffolk)

The Norman army

By contrast with Harold's army, we know quite a lot about
William's. Although the list of those who 'came over with the
Conqueror' grew in later centuries, the names of at least thirty-
five are reliably known. Wace gives a list of no fewer than 117
Norman 'lords' though seventy-four of them are designated by

their lands and not by name. Many of William's soldiers were young men, the sons of great families, out to make a name for themselves. At about forty, Duke William was probably one of the oldest men present. His army contained a high proportion of professional fighting men, the cream of northern France, and, despite their youth, they had much experience in the kind of low-level warfare of raids and sieges that characterised Normandy and its neighbouring provinces. None of them, however, had seen anything like the long shield-wall at Hastings. The army marched in three main units which, as General Fuller pointed out, is reminiscent of the threefold division of a Roman legion. In the lead were lightly armed archers, crossbowmen and slingers, analogous with the Roman *hastati* or missile-hurlers. On the Tapestry, most of the Norman archers are small men that look like boys. This might be an allusion to their inferior status, or it may be that, like the *hastati*, Norman archers were indeed mostly young men on the lowest rungs of a military career. Next came the heavy infantry in mail hauberks carrying spears. There are hints in the sources that these 'steady' troops were older, more experienced men, similar to the *principes* of the legion. Behind them trotted the Norman elite, the *milites* or knights, all mounted and organised into *conroi* or squadrons, each with their own distinctive pennant. On the battlefield, the army seems to have formed into line maintaining the same threefold rank within each division, archers foremost with the horses whinnying in the rear behind a forest of spears. The army also included non-combatants: carters, servant-boys fetching and carrying, perhaps military engineers in charge of fortifications, and priests, some of whom might have doubled as leeches or medical men. Like the Saxons, Norman priests could be active on the battlefield. Bishop Odo rode into battle carrying his mace of office. Other men of the cloth present included Geoffrey, bishop of Coutances and one Remigius, later to be made bishop of Dorchester.

The backbone of Duke William's army was Norman. Many of the great families of Normandy were represented: Eu, Evreux, Giffard, Beaumont, Warenne, Montfort, Grandmesnil and many more. With the Normans came sizeable contingents from the neighbouring provinces of Brittany, Ponthieu and Maine, represented by a nominee of the ruling count, or, at least in the case of Boulogne, by the count himself. These counties were more or less allied to Normandy, and had a share in William's great enterprise. Family ties and the prospect of reward brought aid from further afield, from the Île de France, Flanders and Aquitaine, and, according to one source, even knights from Salerno and Sicily, all eager to cash in on what his chaplain calls William's 'well known generosity'. Typical among William's mercenaries were Garnier le Riche and Simon de Senlis, young French knights who made a living from hiring out their services. The contract bought the small private army of each knight.

The Norman army was divided into three divisions. On the left were the Bretons, led by Alan the Red ('Rufus') of Penthièvre, a cousin of the ruling count and related to William by marriage. Alan the Red - he had a brother named Alan the Black, perhaps an allusion to the colour of their hair - was in constant attendance at the Norman court, and was to be richly rewarded with over 400 confiscated manors, including the 'Honour of Richmond' in Yorkshire. He was the founder of Richmond Castle. The Normans evidently looked down on the Bretons as undisciplined and untrustworthy. William of Poitiers regarded them as little better than brigands, adding that they were addicted to feuds and polygamy. Instead of living in settlements like decent folk, they lived off the land like nomads. Even Lanfranc, William's civilised archbishop, once described the Bretons as 'scum'. Hence, when we read that the Breton knights were the first to turn and run at Hastings, we should bear in mind this evident prejudice: running away in panic is exactly what the eager but unreliable Bretons could be expected to do. The French said the same about the Normans.

The men from Maine under Haimer or Aimeri of Thouars fought with the Bretons. He too was a kinsman of the Duke, and, like the Bretons, was experienced in war, fighting with them against their common enemy, the Angevins. Here again, there may have been tensions. Robert Wace had heard a story of an unnamed knight of Maine who refused to surrender up his horse to William during one of the occasions when the Duke had lost his mount. This was seen as an act of cowardice, if not disloyalty; 'a blow from the Duke's hand brought the disobedient rider to the ground'. This story also serves to point up the contrasting conduct of Count Eustace of Boulogne, who in similar circumstances willingly parted with his own horse.

The centre division was commanded by Duke William himself with his half-brothers Odo and Robert, together with the Norman

NORMAN LINES

View of the field from the Norman centre close to one of the 'stew ponds' later built along the course of the brook.

elite. Very probably it was the largest, being the one that faced King Harold and his housecarls on the steepest part of the ridge. It was perhaps as large as both wings put together. Always close to William was the papal banner, borne, according to tradition, by Turstin (or Thurstan), son of Rollo. On the right were the Flemings, Poitevins and French, stiffened by Normans like the brave Robert de Beaumont, and under the command of William's seneschal and boon companion, William fitzOsbern, as well as the more uncertain Eustace of Boulogne. Eustace had long nurtured ambitions in England, having married a sister of Edward the Confessor, and seems to have had his own agenda. By coincidence or not, William's army was arranged geographically, from Brittany on the left to Flanders and Boulogne on the right. Men fought by their neighbours, no doubt in a spirit of comradeship and rivalry.

In terms of numbers we are again in the dark, although we can safely discount William of Poitiers' theatrical estimate of 60,000. The concensus, which is no more than a guess, is that William's expedition numbered about 10,000 men, which, leaving aside sailors, servants, cooks and other non-combatants, amounted to about 7,500 fighting men and between 2,000 and 3,000 horses.

View of Battle Abbey and its terrace from the west of the Norman position, on ground pounded over by the Breton cavalry.

BRETON CAVALRY

However, plausible estimates go as high as 14,000 men and 10,000 combatants. It would help if we knew how many ships there were. A Ship List possibly compiled between 1067 and 1072 contains a total of 776 ships provided by fourteen magnates, which is in the same order as the chronicler Wace's figure of 696 ships. The smallish Norman ships on the Bayeux Tapestry hold between ten and twenty men each, less for the horse transports, and so the expedition could have been well in excess of 10,000 men. A tentative breakdown of William's army would be 2,000 horse, 4,000 heavy infantry and 1,500 archers and crossbowmen. The unusual length of the battle suggests that the sides were fairly evenly matched.

The moment

It is the moment of destiny. Two great armies face each other across 400 yards of marsh and scrubby hillside. On the outcome of the next few hours lies the future of England. We have reached, in Emily Brontë's words, 'the now, the here, through which all future plunges to the past'. In the subliminal space between thought and action, a hero might be allowed a moment of calm and release. Emily Brontë believed that in his last hours, Harold moved from mere kingship to immortality: war had transcended him.

'In peace he would doubtless have been, like other princes seated on a tranquil throne, a nothing, a wretch entombed within his palace, sunk in pleasures, deceived by flatterers, knowing that of all his people he is the least free... Harold on the field of battle, without palace, without courtiers, without pomp, without luxury, having only the sky of his country above him for a roof, and that land beneath his feet, which he will only abandon with his life - Harold, surrounded by that crowd of devoted hearts, the representatives of millions more, all entrusting to him their safety, their liberty, and their existence as a people... As visible to men as to his Creator, the soul divine shines in his eyes; a multitude of human passions awake there, but they are exalted, sanctified, almost deified. That courage has no rashness, that pride has no arrogance, that indignation has no injustice, that assurance has no presumption. Let the enemy come! still the victory is Harold's. He feels that all must retreat, fall, before him. To him who fights in defence of his native soil, the stroke of death is the stroke given to the slave, to liberate him, and set him free.'

In her novel, *The Golden Warrior* (1948), Hope Muntz has Harold offering a few 'Agincourt' words to his followers. As in Henry V's army, there had been grumblings at Harold's stand-fast strategy. The fyrd, packed like fish in a barrel behind the line of housecarls, felt dishonoured. Standing still was no way to fight a battle.

'Hear me, men,' (Harold) said. 'If I should build a sea-wall, would I set a single line of stones to guard the land?'

A man of Romney shouted: 'No, but a rampart, King'.

'Aye,' said Harold, 'behind the dressed stones an earthen rampart. Both must hold, or else the sea bursts in and the land drowns. I set you here, Housecarles and Thegns and fyrd, to stem this flood. Mailed warriors and levies, ye are one; the wall and rampart of this Kingdom. Stand then, have patience. Those that fled [some of Harold's men had deserted] shall hear your glory and find courage. It is not William's horsemen or his archers that shall save him then. He fears us now. His ships are beached, lest his men fly. This day is a beginning.'

When the noise abated, he said again:

'By all that you hold dear, I bid you stand. He will feign flight and try to draw you down. By that alone can he succeed; for if you go, what can you do against mailed horsemen? Can stones and earth unjoined hold back the sea? Whether the days of Ethelred must come again or whether we shall leave our children peace and a proud memory, it lies upon the issue of this field.'

They heard him grimly, but they saw him smile.

'We gave the Northmen four-and-twenty ships,' he said. 'How many for the Normans?'

They answered with a roar of laughter: 'Let the bastards swim'.

'Aye, let them swim,' said Harold. 'God be with you.'

As for Duke William, his own former chaplain was in no doubt that he made an exceptionally fine speech, but admits he had not heard it. Nevertheless he goes on to tell his listeners what William might have said. There was no way open for retreat. Their way was blocked by the English, while behind them lay only the sea. But under William they had always been victorious. The time had come for the knights to set the seal on their great reputations, their glorious past. The English had no prowess in battle to match theirs. They must be daring, they must never yield, and in a short time they would rejoice in victory. Thus runs William of Poitiers, rather spoiling his story by minimising the dangers. It was about nine in the morning of the 14 of October, on the feast day of St Callixtus, the martyred pope.

Timetable of the Battle of Hastings

The exact times in most cases are approximate. The only reliably recorded facts are that the battle began at nine in the morning and went on until dusk - about nine hours.

7 am: Warned of Harold's position on Caldbec Hill by scouts, William's army advances from Hastings. They arrive on Telham Hill at about 8 am.

8.30: Harold's army deploy along the ridge. William's moves into the valley where it deploys into three divisions facing the English.

9 am: Taillefer juggles and chants before the army. The battle begins with the advance of William's archers.

9.30: The Norman cavalry attack.

9.45: The crisis: William's men fall back, pursued by part of the Harold's army. Gyrth and Leofwine fall.

10 am: William rallies his men.

10.30: The Normans counter-attack, over-running isolated groups of English with the cavalry. The hillock incident.

11 am: The armies regroup.

12 noon: Fighting resumes with another infantry assault followed by the first feigned flight.

2 pm: A second successful feigned flight weakens the English army.

4 pm: In a final win-or-lose assault, William orders his archers to fire high, plunging arrows onto the heads of the English. King Harold is wounded in the eye.

4.30: The Normans gain the ridge and begin to roll up the English position.

5 pm: In a last stand around the standard, Harold is killed, and the English army breaks up.

6 pm: The Malfosse incident.

8 pm: William camps on the battlefield.

Chapter 8

HASTINGS: THE MORNING

Battlecries and jugglers

Hastings was a noisy battle. It began with what William of Poitiers describes as an 'awesome baying of trumpets' from both sides. The din of the shouting, he adds, was soon muffled by the clang of weapons and the groans of the dying. The yelling started the moment the armies came in sight of one another. As anyone who has been on a protest march will know, shouting in company makes us all feel a little bit braver. The English set up a chant of 'Ut, ut' (out, out), perhaps accompanied (as in modern re-enactments of the battle) by pounding their shields with the pommel of their swords. Wace preserves some other battle cries, which he renders in cod-English for his French-speaking readers - 'Godemite' meant 'God Almighty!' - and 'Olicrosse' 'Holy Cross'. The latter is an allusion to the Holy Cross of Waltham, a miraculous crucifix which Harold had enshrined at his secular college in Waltham. It is supposed that Harold and the more cultivated sort were of the 'Holy Cross' faction and that the chant of 'Ut, ut' was uttered by the rank and file (though I cannot imagine anyone shouting 'Holy Cross' - in re-enactments it sounds plain embarrassing). It would be surprising if the cries did not involve some more direct abuse of the Normans in general, and William in particular. It was known that he was sensitive to being called 'Bastard' - and one automatically thinks of the great shouts of 'Bastards!' from the Scots at Stirling in the film *Braveheart*.

The Normans are supposed to have confined themselves to pious exclamations, such as *Dex aïe* or *Dex tot poissant* - 'God aid us!' They, too, shouted 'Holy Cross' ('Sainte croix!') as if in mockery: they were referring to the rival cross on the papal banner, which was no doubt meant to diminish Harold's homegrown one. These oaths come from the same slanted source, Robert Wace, that gives the English a night of feasting and the Normans a night of prayer. The chronicler has the sides playing roles he thought suitable, but the reality was probably more like the inchoate roar heard at football matches: the barbarians versus the bastards.

There may also have been singing. William of Malmesbury has

the Normans singing or chanting the *Roman de Rou*, the song of brave Roland facing the Saracens at Roncesvalles. Others, including the *Carmen*, transfer the song to a jongleur or mummer called Taillefer (the name means 'cut-iron'), who also entertained the troops by juggling with a sword, tossing it high in the air. After concluding his party piece, the juggler showed he was also a soldier by overcoming and slaying an Englishman sent out to fight him. This, of course, was immensely encouraging to the Normans. A different version of the story has Taillefer charging suicidally at the English and killing two of them before being himself cut down. The story may be true in its essentials: Duke William's troops would not have been the first or the last to be exhorted and entertained before going into battle. The Swedish army of Gustavus Adolphus held prayer sessions before the Battle of Lützen in 1632, while Cromwell's Ironsides sang psalms at Dunbar in 1650. However Taillefer had no need to get himself killed. A pointless gesture by the minstrel would have been akin to strapping Vera Lynn into a Spitfire, and was not really necessary.

The battle begins

No one mentions what the weather was like at Hastings on 14 October 1066. Scribes of other medieval battles point out the warm afternoon sunshine at Stamford Bridge, the sudden thunderstorm at Evesham, or the thick morning mist at Barnet. The Battle of Hastings was evidently fought on one of those meteorologically forgettable late autumn days. It was neither hot nor cold, nor did it rain. On the ridge, there was a breeze brisk enough to fly the Wessex dragon banner. Otherwise it was

Norman horse charge the Saxon shield-wall at Hastings. Note the lone Saxon archer. At this stage in the battle, the main weapons are missiles arrows, javelins and sundry projectiles, including small axes and a mace.

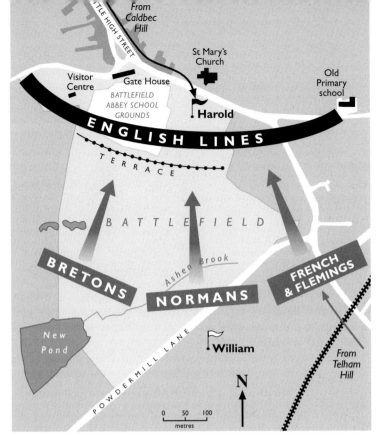

probably one of those nondescript October days, cool, dry and cloudy. Perfect weather for a battle, in fact.

The Battle of Hastings began at Terce, the third hour, or nine o'clock in the morning. The historian E.A. Freeman remarked that all medieval battles start at one of the church hours, that is, to the sound of church bells. William's archers and crossbowmen moved forward and loosed their arrows. Eleventh century archers would halt at a particular point, perhaps fifty yards from

A Saxon shield-wall, ready to receive the enemy. At Hastings the shields were mostly kite-shaped rather than round, and the front line was armed with spears and missiles rather than swords. The Viking Society

the enemy line, dumping their quivers in front of them and commence firing. Harold's housecarls ducked behind their shields as the 'iron-storm' clattered over their heads, stuck in shields, or landed, spent, behind the lines. The opening storm was not, by most accounts, very effective. The archers were shooting uphill at a relatively narrow target. However, Baudri describes how it seemed to the English that death was falling from the sky. The *Carmen* dwells on its fearful effects, 'transfixing bodies with their shafts', while the crossbowmen 'destroyed the shields as if by a hail-storm, shattered them by countless blows'.

The English shield-wall endured the storm, crouched beneath their shields. Even as the archers shouldered their empty quivers and withdrew, William's heavy infantry were moving forward in

close formation. They had only a short toil up a scrubby slope in their heavy hauberks to engage with the English, and as they neared the crest of the hill they were met with volleys of close-range missiles: javelins, light throwing-axes and maces, and slingstones. On the Tapestry a solitary English archer, dwarfed by the tall housecarls, bends his bow. The Normans halted a short distance from the English ranks and hurled their own javelins. Then they closed with the tall men of the shield-wall. William of Poitiers describes the ferocity of the English, 'each man fighting in his own way', some wielding makeshift clubs or pitchforks, others dealing savage blows with their axes, which could slice through shields and armour as if they were satin. The housecarls must have opened ranks to allow themselves room to swing their axes. On the Tapestry, however, the emphasis is on missiles. The fallen bodies in the lower panel are nearly all transfixed by javelins or spears through the neck, breast or back; just one, presumably an Englishman, is pierced by arrows in the face and leg. Only a little later do the severed heads and arms of axe casualties start to

An artist's impression of the moment when Duke William rallied his men and countercharged the Saxon fyrd as they broke ranks to pursue the fleeing enemy.

appear. In the written sources, the main weapons are swords, but on the Tapestry only one attacking knight, right at the back, brandishes a sword at this stage. So long as the English were in closed ranks behind a fence of spears and a rampart of shields, they were out of a sword's reach. This weapon probably stayed in its scabbard until the knights were able to catch the enemy in the open.

None of the sources have much to say about the Norman infantry, even though they probably comprised more than half of William's army. Not a single one of them is shown unambiguously on the Bayeux Tapestry. Perhaps it was a matter of status ~ the men that mattered were all on horseback. Possibly it is also a sign of a disappointing performance on the battlefield. At first, the infantry were unable to breach the English shield-wall, thus leaving the Norman cavalry to face the dreadful prospect of taking on an unbeaten enemy in a strong defensive position.

And here they come, in support of the still-engaged infantry, pounding uphill on their little horses, the feared Norman cavalry. William's squadrons spurred forward through the marsh and onwards up the hill, probably breaking into a canter. They rode in loose formation, the men standing in the stirrups, holding the reins with their shield-arm, clutching a sloped lance with the other. As they reached the English line, now closed again to receive the charge, the knights used their lances to thrust at bare English faces and necks. The shock of the cavalry was broken by the slope, which approaches ten degrees or more at the centre of the ridge where the dragon banner flew. They faced ferocious resistance from spearmen and axemen, who occasionally broke ranks to pick off a struggling horseman up to fifty yards away.

It was the Normans who broke. First the battered infantry drew back, followed by the Breton knights and other auxiliaries on the left flank. Soon almost the whole battle-line was falling back in some disorder. This might have been the time when a rumour spread that William had fallen. Such news would have been devastating. Afterwards, everyone remembered the moment when William, in fact very much alive, pulled back his helmet and bellowed at the panicking knights in his harsh, cracked voice. Riding into their path, he blocked their way with his lance and gestured threateningly;

'Look at me!' Poitiers makes him yell above the din.

'I am still alive, and with God's help I shall win! What

A re-enactment of close-order combat with axes and swords. Several chroniclers describe the crush at Hastings, with ranks so close that the dead remained standing. The Viking Society

lunacy makes you turn in flight? What retreat is open to you if you run? They will drive you on and slaughter you! You have it in your power to cut them down like a flock of sheep. You are giving up victory and fame which should last forever. If you keep on, not a single one of you will escape death!'

The scene is shown, out of sequence, on the Tapestry, William turning wild-eyed in his saddle, helmet thrown back, but brandishing not a lance but his mace of office. A moustached Eustace of Boulogne points frantically towards him: HERE IS DUKE WILLIAM! This may be an allusion to an incident recorded

'Here is William!' Count Eustace, bearing the papal banner, points as the Duke rallies his men.

by the *Carmen*, in which Count Eustace offered his own mount to William, who had been unhorsed.

The Tapestry also shows half-brother Odo in action at this point, riding up on his white horse to encourage ('confortat') and rally a number of his young knights, described as *'pueros'* or 'boys'. Who were these 'boys'? Possibly squires or apprentice warriors under Bishop Odo's tutelage, though Robert Wace had heard that they were baggage boys. Like Abbot Aelfwig of Winchester, Odo had evidently come to Hastings at the head of an armed retinue. But Odo's prominence on the Tapestry is due to his position as its patron and Bishop of Bayeux. In the campaign, his wealth mattered more than his military talents.

With William's harangue ringing in their ears, the knights regained their confidence and managed to form up again in some sort of order. The Duke himself led them back into battle. At this point, their fortune changed dramatically. Somehow the Normans were able to encircle and isolate some of the English right wing on a wooded hillock. On the Tapestry the latter are armed with spears, clubs and shields, but without mail or helmets. Two have fallen in the assault, and a third, fleeing one set of horsemen, is about to be trampled down from the opposite direction. A bearded figure, perhaps their leader, stands beneath a pollarded tree with his hand to his face, either shouting or scanning the distance

Norman knights flounder in the mire below Senlac ridge. The pointed things in the water have been interpreted as sharp stakes planted by the crafty Saxons, but more likely they are the designer's attempt at marsh vegetation.

A group of ill-armed Saxons are cornered on a hillock. Norman efforts to pick them off are impeded by marshy ground at its foot.

perhaps for signs of rescue. One of the Norman knights has taken a tumble: his horse flounders in the mud while a comrade catches hold of its saddle straps. But the English are plainly getting the worst of it. They were slaughtered to a man, says William of Poitiers. Not one of them regained the English line.

The hillock episode is probably true. There is a plausible candidate for the hillock in the ridge of land that projects from the western end of the ridge towards what is now the largest fishpond. It is sandy at its summit, and crowned with gorse. By the usual interpretation, the fyrd had broken ranks to pursue the fleeing Bretons, but were cut off and surrounded by the Norman counterattack. Some perished in the marsh, while others regained higher ground for their last stand. Who they were, no one knows. Perhaps they were men from the west, from Berkshire and elsewhere, for the fyrd of Essex and Kent were apparently present to the end, and were praised for their steadfastness.

The *Carmen* tells another story, this time from the perspective of the Frenchmen on the right wing of William's army. They too retreated, but 'versed in stratagems, skilled in warfare', their flight was only a ruse. The English peasants (*rustica gens*), rejoicing and believing they had won, pursued the French with

Hillock

Is this the hillock of Hastings? Near the western end of Senlac ridge a spur of sandy ground projects towards the valley where the New Pond is today.

naked swords. With their fellows on the opposite wing, they 'vied to be the first to slaughter the scattered enemy in various ways'. But the result was the same. A large number - the *Carmen* estimates 'the accursed rabble' at 10,000, or a sixth of the English army - were slaughtered in the open, 'as meek sheep fall before the ravening lion'.

The implication, which is most explicit in the late, untrustworthy account of the battle by Wace, is that the fyrd

Alternative site of the hillock, a modest rise between New Pond and Senlac Hill.

HILLOCK

The New Pond, built in 1815 on the western part of the field where the Bretons formed up to provide water for a gunpowder mill.

disobeyed orders and were left to their fate. To try to rescue them would reinforce error. But another possibility which has gained favour recently is that the episode was part of a general advance which went disastrously wrong. The repulsion of the Norman horse was perhaps the one moment when King Harold could have won the Battle of Hastings. That the English were capable of attack as well as defense they had shown at Fulford and Stamford Bridge, admittedly against an enemy that had chosen, like them, to fight on foot. One of those who argued that this is what Harold should have done, but unaccountably failed to do, was Professor David Douglas, the biographer of William the Conqueror. Until Hastings, Harold's generalship had always been to go onto the offensive when circumstances merited it. As we have seen, this was his plan at Hastings too, until forced onto the defensive by William's advance. Stephen Murillo has interpreted a puzzling passage in the Bayeux Tapestry as evidence that Harold did in fact order a general advance. It is found in the section - a significant one in terms of prominence and length - which shows Harold's brothers, Gyrth and Leofwine, fighting and dying together. The incident is placed immediately after the opening stages of the battle, and, by complete contrast, shows a scene of open fighting. The scene takes place as part of a sequence from the opening charge to the hillock incident. The clear interpretation is that the English had counter-attacked, abandoning their defensive formation on the ridge and pursuing the enemy towards the stream. Murillo's hypothesis is that Gyrth and Leofwine were killed in front of the Saxon army just as the advance was getting underway. The unlucky fall of the brothers would account for its sudden collapse. If so, the wings of the army might not have known about their fate, and continued to advance. At any rate, the Normans were able to take speedy advantage of the disorder. If we had an account of the battle from the English side, it might well have picked this episode as the turn of the tide, in which the battle changed from one of attack and counter-attack to a grim battle of attrition. The English could now rely only on endurance. Victory might still be theirs if reinforcements arrived, but they had first to survive hours of assault without breaking. They were condemned to a defensive battle, leaving the initiative to the enemy.

The fate of Gyrth and Leofwine

The Battle of Hastings eliminated not only the king, but both of his surviving mature brothers. The *Anglo-Saxon Chronicle* recognises the extent of the disaster in recording the death of all three by name, as well as 'many [other] good men'. A modern comparison might be with the Kennedy dynasty in America. The assassination of the President was shocking enough, but imagine the reaction if the assassin had killed not only Jack, but also Bobby and Ted in the same moment! In an instant, the Godwin dynasty, the effective rulers of England for as long as most could remember, was wiped out as a political force.

Most modern accounts gloss over the death of Gyrth and Leofwine as if it were a minor incident in the battle. However, the designer of the Bayeux Tapestry would have disagreed. Immediately after the dramatic opening cavalry charge, the Tapestry shows us a vivid and violent scene of hand-to-hand fighting in which Gyrth and Leofwine lead the English side. A tall figure with long moustaches identified as Gyrth levels his lance at an incoming mounted Norman who, uniquely on the Tapestry, is couching his own lance, aiming at his opponent's neck. In the next, what is probably also intended to be Gyrth reels backwards, struck in the breast by a lance. 'Lewine' (Leofwine) is identified as the slim, beardless figure first shown swinging an axe, then knocked flying by charging horses. The prominence given to

The death of Leofwine (left) and Gyrth ('GYRÐ'), the brothers of Harold.

their deaths suggests that this, far from being incidental, was a crucial moment in the battle. The implication, strengthened by the next scene of horses flailing in the marsh, is that the English had advanced down the hill from their original positions, pursuing the retreating Norman horse.

The *Carmen* preserves a different story in which Gyrth is slain by William himself, who evidently mistook him for his brother, King Harold:

> 'Harold's brother, Gyrth by name, born of a royal line, was undaunted by the face of the lion [i.e. William]: poising a javelin, he hurled it from afar with a strong arm. The flying weapon wounded the body of [his] horse, and forced the duke to fight on foot, but reduced to a foot-soldier, he fought yet better, for he rushed upon the young man [Gyrth was in fact about the same age as William] like a snarling lion. Hewing him limb from limb, he shouted at him: "Take the crown you have earned from us! If my horse is dead, thus I requite you - as a common soldier!"

As in his story of Harold's fall, the author of the *Carmen* may have adapted the story from *The Iliad*, notably the killing of Hector by Achilles. By making William personally bludgeon Gyrth to the ground, he makes a moral point: The 'deserved crown' which Gyrth (standing in for Harold) has earned from the Normans

127

turns out to be the metal blade smashing into his head! It is a moment of retributive irony, strengthened by the *quid pro quo* exchange of Gyrth's life for William's horse. Attempts to construe the *Carmen* as modern war-reporting miss the poetry and moral lessons of eleventh century writing. What the poet does is to turn the bare fact of Gyrth's fate into an appropriate piece of theatre.

According to William of Poitiers, the bodies of the brothers were found near the king's, implying that they died at a late stage in the battle, in the fighting around the king's standard. The statement has been taken to mean that the three stood together at Hastings. But if, on the contrary, Gyrth and Leofwine were slain early on in the battle, their bodies could have been brought there at the king's order. Their housecarls, tied by bonds of livelihood as well as loyalty, were accustomed to stand and fight over the body of a fallen lord, as they did at the Battle of Maldon over the headless body of ealdorman Byrhtnoth. The death of his brothers may be one reason why King Harold stayed in the field to the bitter end, when he could, without loss of honour, have escaped to fight another day. The loss of three brothers in less than a month might well have produced a mood of grim fatalism in the king.

Chapter 9

HASTINGS: THE AFTERNOON

The battle of attrition and the feigned retreats

Partly through the medium of the Bayeux Tapestry, but also because of the way the sources are written, the first phase of the Battle of Hastings is presented as a series of tableaux: the exchange of missiles, the charge of the Norman horse, the retreat of the Bretons, William's intervention, and the encirclement of the fyrd on their hillock. All of this might have taken place in the space of an hour, perhaps two hours, bringing the time to late morning. Yet the Battle of Hastings went on until dusk, at about six in the evening. What happened in the long hours between the elimination of the hillock group and the collapse of the English army? What exactly was the Norman's battle-winning plan?

According to William of Poitiers, it was the tactic of the feigned retreat. He admits that the flight of the morning had not been feigned but was real. The Normans fled, 'their shields covered their backs', relates the *Carmen*, not without a certain French *schadenfreude*. By luck and William's generalship, the incident had been turned to their advantage, for it exposed the English weaknesses of indiscipline and lack of mobility.

'Seeing that it would be impossible for them to overcome, without great loss to themselves, such a numerous enemy

This 'Table Mount' makes the modest incline of Senlac ridge appear like a mountainside!

which offered a cruel resistance,' relates Poitiers, 'the Normans and their allies turned their backs, pretending to take flight.'

Historians have long been divided over whether the feigned retreats at Hastings were a deliberate *ruse de guerre*, or whether the story was invented later to mask a more chaotic battle involving real retreats. Among the doubters was Colonel Charles Lemmon who considered feigned retreat as tactically impossible: it 'would demand that every man taking part in it had to know when to retreat, how far to retreat and when to turn round and fight back' (Lemmon, 1966). Moreover the movements would need to be carefully synchronised or the result would be disastrous. In the heat of the battle it would be impossible. Furthermore, 'a military maxim, evolved after long years of experience in warfare, that "troops once committed to the attack cannot be made to change direction"'.

On the other hand, there is plentiful evidence that feigned flight was used by steppe horsemen like the Magyars and the Alans, and that others, notably the Byzantines, copied it. It is even mentioned in a manual on military tactics by the Byzantine Emperor, Leo the Wise. Moreover the Normans seem to have used feigned retreat at least twice before Hastings: at Arques, in 1053, and at Messina in Sicily in 1060. The commander at Arques, Walter Giffard, was present at Hastings, as were some who had fought in Sicily. Finally, it is hard to dismiss the near-contemporary witness of William of Poitiers and the *Carmen* of Hastings that feigned retreat was successfully used at Hastings, especially as both concede that the Normans were beaten in the opening assault. William of Malmesbury, generally a level-headed commentator, believed not only that feigned retreat was used but that it turned the battle in Duke William's favour.

All the same, we would like to know exactly how it was done, and why the English repeatedly fell for it. There would be nothing inherently difficult about a unit of Norman or Breton horse acting in unison: these were men that practically lived on horseback, and in each other's company. We could imagine a squadron countering up to the English line, and then lead horseman performing a 'roll back' manoevre, turning his steed on it's heels and riding back without losing speed. The rest would follow the leader, for, as herd animals, horses like to follow one another. In this way, groups of excited Englishmen might have been 'teased off the ridge'. But what William of Poitiers seems to be saying, in a confused passage, is that the feigned retreat involved not isolated squadrons but the whole Norman army. It happened at a time when the 'barbarian' English still felt time was on their side, and were hurling abuse at the Normans, 'threatening to overrun them without more ado'. By pretending to retreat, a whole mass of Englishmen, 'thinking to harass those who were running away', was drawn down into the valley only to be cut off, surrounded and massacred in the same way as their compatriots earlier in the day.

William of Poitiers claims that feigned retreat was used twice, but does not describe the second occasion. One explanation may be that the original retreat may have been in part feigned. A little-used English source by the Lincolnshire cleric, Geffrey Gaimer, dwells upon the effective role played by Alan of Brittany at Hastings. The Bretons regarded the Dark Age Alan tribe as their ancestors (hence the popularity among their rulers of the name 'Alan'), and continued to use the same tactics. The *Carmen* states that the Bretons and French were trying out a well-tried-and-tested tactic. It was the Normans, in the middle, who really did run away, only to be halted by threats from their furious and red-faced leader. This would make Poitiers' remark that 'twice the same trick was used' more understandable. Perhaps, for once, the embarrassing truth escaped the chaplain's editing of the facts.

The defeat of the English

The afternoon seems to have passed in a series of assaults on the weakening English position. The Normans 'attacked with the greatest vigour', writes William of Poitiers. The English army, though shorn of its wings, still inspired fear and was very difficult to break through and surround. The Norman attacks burst against the English rock. In a series of loaded statements, Poitiers goes on:

> 'The English weakened, and, as if they admitted their wrongdoing by defeat itself, they now undertook their punishment. The Normans shot arrows, wounded and transfixed men. The dead, as they tumbled to the ground, showed more sign of motion than the living. Even the lightly wounded could not escape, but perished under the dense heap of their companions. So fortune concurred in William's triumph by hastening it'.

A similar passage in the *Carmen* alludes to the terrible vengeance meted out to the English for fighting in a lost cause:

> 'O Ruler of Heaven, thou who art tender and pitiful towards us and by divine will rulest all things, what destruction the surviving band of English suffered! Then pity died and cruelty triumphed, life perished, savage death raged, and the sword ran wild! Where Mars holds sway, no man shows mercy.'

Heroic actions from various Norman knights were remembered long afterwards. Robert fitzErneis, a knight from Rouen, led a force of twenty men to seize the English standard. The attempt failed, and fitzErneis was cut down by a housecarl's axe as he caught hold of the dragon banner. Was this in fact a 'snatch squad', specially deputed to attack the English command post,

The battle in late afternoon, with the English line broken in several places and perhaps fragmenting. William's archers provide covering fire for the infantry and horse.

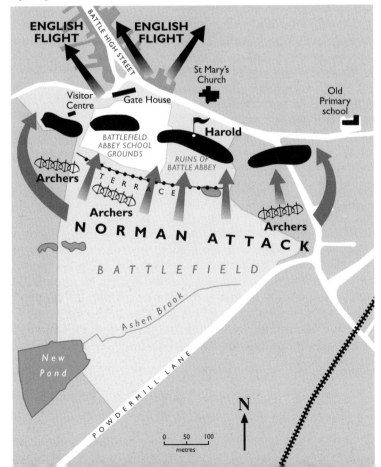

The last few feet of the Bayeaux Tapestry shows the Saxons clearly getting the worst of it as Norman archers maintain a flanking fire. Earlier on, the casualties are shown as about even.

and perhaps kill King Harold himself? The tactic was not unknown in medieval warfare. Harald Hardrada seems to have used such means at Fulford and Stamford Bridge, putting himself at their head, and a similar detachment was under orders to reach, and kill, Simon de Montfort at the Battle of Evesham.

Another mysterious episode involved an Englishman known only as the 'son of Helloc', perhaps a French version of 'Haveloc'. This man is said to have lain in wait for Duke William, and cast his javelin at him, but succeeded only in wounding his horse. The Duke went sprawling, but, springing to his feet and;

> 'seeing the author of the crime lurking at a distance in the press, he rushed forthwith to destroy him. Cutting through the groin with a thrust of his right hand and a merciless sword-stroke, he spilt his entrails on the ground'.

The site of the Abbey church. The outline of cloisters survive on the wall of Battle Abbey school, on the site of the abbot's palace. Some of the most desperate fighting took place here.

The Tapestry has a scene of a Norman seizing an unarmed man by the hair, clearly about to put him to the sword. It has been suggested that this may be an allusion to the Haveloc story, although the word woven above the unfortunate man is, by coincidence, 'HAROLDO' ('AND THOSE HAVE FALLEN WHO WERE WITH HAROLD').

There is a sense of growing desperation and violence in the last scenes of the Tapestry. Housecarls, who seem immortal at the start of the battle, are now shown being struck down by the swords and lances of the Norman cavalry. It scarcely needs the legend 'AND THOSE HAVE FALLEN WHO WERE WITH HAROLD'. The archers in the lower panel have been busy, and the shields of the English bristle with arrows. How the archers managed to replenish their quivers at this stage is not clear. Perhaps, having pushed back the English line, they were able to scavenge spent arrows from the battlefield. Or perhaps fresh supplies of arrows had arrived from the ships. We can imagine a short but effective storm of arrows falling on the crushed ranks of the English, followed by the shock of the cavalry assault. Bit by bit, the English were worn down, and the Normans started to penetrate their lines, at last gaining a foothold on the ridge.

It was perhaps now, as the late afternoon sunlight slanted across the piles of bodies, that King Harold was killed, with or without an arrow in the eye. In the *Carmen*, Harold, in his last moments, performs prodigies of valour, hewing down the Normans now investing his hilltop position. This story is probably intended to magnify the Normans' fame in overcoming the hero and winning the battle. At this stage in the battle, the attention turns to Harold and William personally. Both were great warriors, but, since the sources are Norman and French, William is of course the greater, Achilles to Harold's Hector, Aeneus to the latter's Turnus. His chaplain claims that Duke William surpassed even the bravest of his knights:

'His leadership in battle was noble, preventing men from fleeing, inspiring courage in others, sharing danger, more often ordering his men to follow him than to advance... Three horses were killed under him. Three times he intrepidly leapt to the ground and hastened to avenge the death of his warhorse. This showed his quickness, his strength of mind and body. The fury of his sword pierced shields, helmets and hauberks; he struck down several soldiers with his shield alone... He helped and rescued many men.'

The *Carmen* differs only in claiming William had only two horses killed from under him, but the picture of a mighty warrior is much the same: 'At the appearance of the duke the trembling host fell back, as soft wax melts away in the face of fire. With drawn sword he hewed to pieces helms and shields, and even his war-horse slew many'; presumably by trampling them.

Clearly there must have been some justification for such stories, and we need not doubt that William was a prominent figure on the battlefield and the architect of the Norman victory. All the same, the William of the Bayeux Tapestry is presented more plausibly as an orthodox commander, giving orders and haranguing his fleeing men, but never shown actually fighting. In contrast to his knights, but like his priestly half-brother Odo, he carries no shield, and in his hand is no sword but a harmless wooden mace of office. It was necessary for the sources to present a valorous, martial William outdoing the great men of ancient myth. But there is an air of cliché about William's supposed exploits, and even in Poitiers' account, the emphasis is on William's qualities as an inspiring leader of men rather than the man who more or less singlehandedly won the Battle of Hastings. He seems to take on two roles: the commander with his staff, and the embodiment of the Norman army. When the *Carmen* has him personally killing Harold, Gyrth and several thousand others, his audience no doubt understood it in a poetical sense: they were killed by Normans, William was the leader of the Normans, therefore William killed them.

Another view of the levelled ground near Harold's command post. Monk's dormitory (left) and Battle Abbey school in the background.

This inscribed slab marks the position of the high altar of the Abbey, which in turn stood on the exact place where Harold's body and fallen banners of Saxon England were found after the battle.

By the time Harold was slain and his standard overthrown, the shield-wall had crumbled and the English line may have shrunk to a circular phalanx of men in the vicinity of the present-day abbey. On the Tapestry only two men stand by the king, his standard-bearer and a lone housecarl. The death of King Harold, so vividly shown on the Bayeux Tapestry, so closely described in the *Carmen* and other sources, though significantly not by William of Poitiers, is a contentious subject that it will be treated separately below. However, his loss effectively ended the battle and began a *sauve qui peut*, as the English fled the field. As the *Carmen* put it, 'The flying rumour "Harold is dead!" spread through the fray'. At that news proud hearts were tamed by fear: 'The English refused battle. Vanquished they besought mercy; despairing of life, they fled from death'. The impression given elsewhere is that the housecarls fought to the death, while it was the fyrd, or some of them, that fled. No housecarls flee or beg for mercy on the Bayeux Tapestry: they are last seen fighting and falling with sword and axe amid a thicket of Norman lances. Even as Harold receives his death wound, scavengers were at work, stripping bodies of their coats of mail, or collecting weapons and shields. In the last surviving section of the Tapestry, five mounted Normans, including an archer, pursue the English as they flee into the forest. Three of the English have found mounts, which they lash frantically in their haste. One unfortunate has entangled himself

Close up of the inscription.

THE TRADITIONAL SITE OF
THE HIGH ALTAR OF BATTLE ABBEY
FOUNDED TO COMMEMORATE
THE VICTORY OF DUKE WILLIAM
ON 14 OCTOBER 1066
THE HIGH ALTAR WAS PLACED TO MARK
THE SPOT WHERE KING HAROLD DIED

Attacked from front and behind, the weary housecarls fight to the death.

in a thicket (or is he climbing a tree?). Another runs blindly with an arrow sticking from an eye. The last figure on the Tapestry is a poor naked figure apparently hiding in the bushes, peering out at the carnage.

The Death of King Harold

The climactic event of the Battle of Hastings - and the reason why it proved decisive - was, of course, the death of King Harold. The sources all recognise this, and give the event its due prominence. However the accounts of his final moments vary. There is no unanimity about when Harold died. Most say he fell late on in the battle, perhaps shortly before dusk. However, William of Jumiéges, followed by Orderic Vitalis, asserts that he fell 'covered with deadly wounds in the very first coming together of the armies'. This can be dismissed: if it was true, the battle would have been over there and then. As in chess, the fall of the king marks the end of the game. The *Chronicle of Battle Abbey* may well be near the mark in asserting that Harold was slain by a chance blow from an unknown hand. Wace, too, claims that the press around the king was so great that no one knew the identity of the slayer. Of course, the scene everyone knows is on the last but one panel of the Bayeux Tapestry: 'HIC HAROLD: REX: INTERFECTUS: EST' - 'Here King Harold is killed'. Beneath the word HAROLD, a tall figure clutches an arrow, seemingly embedded in his right eye. Under the words 'INTERFECTUS EST', another figure is cut down by a nameless mounted knight and falls like a log, an axe spinning from his nerveless hands. There has been much debate about which of the two figures is meant to be King Harold. The answer, in all probability, is both. Like the panels on the death of Gyrth and Leofwine, the tapestry works like a strip cartoon. Harold, standing beneath his dragon banner, is struck by an arrow. Shortly afterwards he is cut down and finished off by the knight. That this falling figure also once had an arrow in his eye is indicated by a close examination of the Tapestry, which reveals a row of stitching holes. However even this is not completely conclusive, since this part of the Tapestry has been heavily restored. Even so, most scholars now believe that the Tapestry meant to show us the king being wounded and then cut down.

The tradition that Harold was struck in the eye by an arrow was well known to chroniclers writing a generation or two afterwards. The earliest mention is in a history of the Normans by Amatus, a monk of Monte Cassino in Italy, around 1080. William of Malmesbury describes how, after 'Harold fell dead with his brain pierced by a blow from an arrow', the English fled headlong through the night. Writing a century afterwards, Robert Wace elaborates:

'Then it happened that, as it whistled down out of the sky, one of the arrows struck Harold just above his right eye. In great anguish he dragged it out, snapping it in half and throwing it on the ground; but it had put his eye out. He was in great pain from this wound in his head, and he collapsed forward on his shield...'

But how did they know this? Did the Bayeux Tapestry create the story, or were they all repeating what was generally known? Perhaps reports of the eye injury were based on an examination of Harold's corpse. However a different, seemingly incompatible, tradition is preserved by the *Carmen*, which in an ambiguous passage, seems to name Duke William himself as the kingslayer. The *Carmen*'s French audience were treated to a front-seat, blow-by-blow account of the king's last moments:

'[The duke] called Eustace to his side. He handed over the fighting in that sector to the French and moved up to give all the relief that he possibly could to those who were being slaughtered [by Harold]. Ever keen to do his duty, just as if he, too, had been of the race of Hector, Hugh, the noble heir to Ponthieu, went with them. The fourth man was

A classic depiction of Harold's death. Harold has been engraved wearing plate armour and seated on his horse. In fact, he fought on foot surrounded by his housecarls, until he was hacked down.

Is this King Harold? (left) Or is this? (right) And was the fatal arrow on the original tapestry, or a later alteration?

Giffard, who inherited this name from his father. By the use which they made of their weapons, these four between them encompassed the king's death ... With the point of his lance the first [William?] pierced Harold's shield and then penetrated his chest, drenching the ground with his blood, which poured out in torrents. With his sword the second [Eustace] cut off his head, just below where his helmet protected him. The third [Hugh] disembowelled him with his javelin. The fourth [Giffard] hacked off his leg at the thigh and hurled it far away. Struck down in this way, his dead body lay on the ground.'

The *Carmen* seems to be saying that Harold was targetted personally, perhaps in a desperate bid to end the battle. By this stage, the English were weakening and a squadron of picked Norman knights could punch their way through to the royal standard. In this version of events, Harold is still uninjured and unwearied, and needs the efforts of four mounted knights to finish him off. On the Bayeux Tapestry the sword of the anonymous knight striking Harold lies suggestively across the king's thighs, perhaps in the process of chopping his leg off. One modern theory is that the *Carmen*'s reference to a thigh is in fact a euphemism, and that the poor king was in fact emasculated. It is said that the leg-chopper, the headstrong son of Duke William's old friend and councillor Walter Giffard, was stripped of his knighthood and sent home in disgrace, having done a deed that even the Normans found unchivalrous and disgusting. William of Malmesbury had heard a different story. The villain was Ivo of Ponthieu, and he had cut off not the leg but the hands from Harold's corpse.

Interestingly, the best-informed source, William of Poitiers, does not tell us how Harold died. The body of the king, he says, was found on the field afterwards, much mutilated and 'recognised not by any insignia he wore, and certainly not from his features, but by certain distinguishing marks'. There is nothing here about Duke William's participation, which Poitiers was unlikely to omit, unless, perhaps, there was something dishonourable about the way Harold died. All of this speculation overlooks the rather obvious point that if William had personally killed King Harold, he would not have needed to send people to search for the body afterwards.

For what it is worth, I suspect the traditional accounts of Harold's slaying to be based on poetic licence. The *Carmen*'s surgical account has strong overtones of the ritual execution of a traitor. It might also have been poetically or politically appropriate to have the leaders of Normandy, Boulogne and Ponthieu in at the kill. The scene might also have been modelled on the death of Patroclus in *The Iliad*. It would not, in fact, have been possible, in

'And the English have turned in flight'. Some of them have found horses, probably kept in a pound to the rear of their lines. Others hide in trees and bushes.

the heat of the moment, to seek out a man and then systematically behead, disembowel and chop his leg off, not least because the king was protected from head to ankle in the finest mail. By the same token, an eye-wound from a chance arrow - death falling from the sky - might have been construed as a fit punishment for one who was blind to William's claim to be king. The *Battle Abbey chronicle* preserves an interesting story that Harold swore his oath on a reliquary called the Ox's Eye, perhaps the one shown on the Tapestry with a slightly bulging lid. The falling arrow was directed by God as punishment for a foresworn usurper. In this way, the punishment fitted the crime, just as in the death of Biblical characters like Ahab or Jezebel. Even so, Giffard's (or Ivo's) disgrace strikes a different note. Walter Giffard senior was a prominent courtier and companion of the duke, and this story would not have been made up unless the dishonoured Giffard *fils* really had mutilated the fallen king's corpse, presumably after he was dead. And it does seem to be true that the body was hacked and dismembered almost beyond recognition. Harold had reigned for exactly nine months and eight days.

The evening

The horses of the English army were tethered well in the rear, probably somewhere along the line of the present High Street. The fading light and the shelter of nearby woods allowed many men to gallop or slip away into the night. Many wounded dragged themselves into the tangled trackways of the Weald, only to die far from home from loss of blood or exposure. William of Poitiers tells us many died under the trees, and that their pursuers found corpses all along the roads. The Normans gave no quarter even now, and their horse trampled the bodies that lay in their path. The battlefield itself was a scene of utter carnage, with stripped bodies and dead horses scattered over what Poitiers describes as a vast distance, lying in heaps where the fighting had been most intense. As the battle went on, the bodies in the Tapestry margins grew ever more mutilated, ending naked and in pieces - heads, arms, hands and headless torsos.

Around dusk, the English managed to turn the tables on their pursuers in the well-remembered incident of the Malfosse or 'evil ditch'. A group of English made a last stand somewhere north of the battlefield along what Poitiers describes as broken rampart (*vallum*) with a labyrinth of ditches. Who these men were is unknown: perhaps they were a rearguard covering the English retreat, or possibly late arrivals from surrounding villages, bringing with them local knowledge of ambush sites. The Duke riding up and seeing men gathered there in the dark assumed them to be a new force. In Poitiers' version, a group of fifty knights, led by Eustace of Boulogne first encountered this English rearguard and, not liking the look of their entrenchments, had pusillanimously turned back. 'The difficulty of the ground meant that the Normans did not show their usual courage', he explains. Seeing the Duke, Eustace rode up to him and whispered his advice to withdraw at once, predicting instant death if they went on. 'With his manly voice,' William restrained him. At that moment, Eustace was struck between the shoulders by a projectile of some sort and slumped to the ground, blood streaming from his nose and mouth. As the injured count was borne away, William, though armed with only the stump of a broken lance, attacked at once and trampled his adversaries underfoot. This story, of course, has a wholesome moral: victory goes to the brave. It is also a dig at Count Eustace, who had fallen out with William by the time Poitiers was penning his chronicle.

Writing sixty years later, Orderic Vitalis had heard a different version of the incident. Here the Norman horse, galloping in pursuit of the fleeing English, had failed to notice an ancient earthwork hidden by long grass, over which they tumbled 'falling one on top of another in a struggling mass of horses and arms'. One of those who fell here was the noble Engenulf, castellan of Laigle, from whose family Orderic may have got the story. In the *Battle Abbey Chronicle*, the earthwork becomes 'an immense ditch' or 'deep pit' hidden by brambles and thistles, into which the Normans fell headlong and 'died tragically, pounded to pieces'. This place the chronicler knew as the Malfosse.

'Diex Aie!' This monument to the brave of both sides, stands in a corner of the Abbey grounds with the tower of St Mary's church just beyond.

Inside the Malfosse; a steep-walled jungle of trees, bushes and nettles through which the boggy stream bed runs.

The Malfosse has been identified, very plausibly, with a deep gully known as Oakwood Gill (Chevallier 1963), which runs east to west across the London road about a mile north of the battlefield. Hidden from view by bushes, it is easy to imagine how men, riding down from Caldbec Hill in the half-light, would not have noticed the obstacle until they were almost upon it. There, it seems, they were ambushed as the horses reared or plunged over the steep side of the gully. It was probably a minor incident, but such things are often remembered and blown out of proportion. Here, in contrast to the battle scenes, we have a sharp picture: William, with his broken lance, Eustace injured by a mysterious blow, the dangers of the dark and unknown ground.

William returned to the battlefield and established his camp nearby. He spent a restless night, according to the *Carmen*, 'not overcome by sleep, nor suffering himself to dream'. Darkness shrouded the dead - for the moon did not rise until after midnight and remained low. Even so, William of Poitiers has the Duke moved by pity at the heaps of slain, though, he is quick to remind us, the victims were wicked men and it is glorious and praiseworthy to slay a tyrant.

The next day, 15 October, was given over to the burial of the Norman dead. 'After the glorious light of the sun began to shine

The Malfosse today; the 'immense ditch' where Norman knights 'fell on top of one another in a struggling mass'.

and cleanse the world of brooding darkness,' runs the *Carmen* in poetic flight, 'the duke surveyed the field.' The Norman dead were buried in a mass grave ('in the bosom of the earth') at an unknown location, possibly where the abbey later stood. A victory cairn may have been built on Caldbec Hill. Though nothing survives of the monument, the local name 'mountjoy' may well be a reference to it. The uncounted corpses of the English were stripped of anything of value and left to be devoured by worms and wolves, by birds and dogs. According to William of Poitiers, however, anyone who came to the field was given licence to remove their loved ones for burial.

With one exception. The bodies of the three Godwin brothers were found, apparently together. Harold was recognised only with difficulty. According to legend his mangled corpse was found amid heaps of slain by his former common-law wife, Edith Swanneck. She had accompanied the English to Hastings, and awaited the outcome of the battle by an oak tree on Caldbec Hill, known ever afterwards as the Watch Oak. Duke William took personal charge of the funeral arrangements, wrapping the body in fine purple linen and conveying it to his camp at Hastings. The *Carmen* has Harold's mother 'in the toils of overwhelming grief' sending a messenger to the duke entreating him to restore her three sons to her, and offering his weight in gold for Harold's

A Victorian engraving showing Harold's body being identified by his former common-law wife, Edith Swanneck. In the story, she knew it only by certain secret signs.

body. The duke, in fury, rejected both petitions and mockingly swore that he would entrust Harold with guarding the port of Hastings - from under a heap of stones. The body was accordingly buried 'on the high summit of a cliff' by Harold's former friend, the Anglo-Norman William Malet, lord of Graville. The gravestone read:

> You rest here, King Harold, by order of the duke,
> So that you may still be guardian of the shore and sea.

This, says Poitiers, was Harold's punishment for his excessive greed, which had caused the deaths of so many who would never find proper graves. Harold should be made to guard the shore and sea in death as in life. The Normans enjoyed the irony. It was a good jest.

It may, however, be untrue. William of Malmesbury believed that the Conqueror did, in fact, surrender the body to Harold's mother, Gytha, who had it laid in her son's foundation at Waltham Holy Cross. The twelfth-century chronicle of Waltham Abbey claims that the church had sent two canons, Osgod Cnoppe and Aethelric Childemaister, to accompany the king on his campaign, and that it was they who persuaded William to let them have the body. The site of the grave is still marked in the grass, where the high altar of Waltham Abbey stood until the Reformation when the east end of the church was demolished (see page 155).

A fourteenth century chronicler mentions that the tomb bore the king's image. David Hume, the nineteenth century Scottish historian claimed to have discovered a now lost stone at Waltham, bearing the inscription: HIC IACET HAROLDUS INFELIX, (here lies the unfortunate Harold). No one records what happened to the bodies of Harold's brothers, Gyrth and Leofwine. But since they were not under the same anathema as the king, it seems likely that they received a family burial, perhaps in the family vault at Bosham. A stone coffin, excavated from under the chancel arch at Bosham in 1954, contained a much fractured skeleton lacking the skull and a leg. On the basis of similarities with the *Carmen*'s account of the injuries received by King Harold, a local historian, John Pollock, has suggested that these are the bones of Harold himself, though this seems unlikely in view of the well documented claim of Waltham Abbey. It is possible however, that they could belong to one of the brothers.

Chapter 10

AFTERMATH AND VERDICT

Casualties

To the men of 1066, the scale of the defeat could only be explained by the wrath of God. The 'D' Chronicle ascribed it to God's vengeance on the English people for their sins. The apocalypse had been widely predicted the year 1000. Some may have felt the millennium had at last arrived, a little late but with undiluted dread and menace. William of Jumièges considered it was divine recompense for the foul and unjust murder in 1036 of Prince Alfred, brother of Edward the Confessor, arranged, some said, with the connivance of Harold's father, Godwin. No one knew how many Englishmen died at Hastings. For William of Malmesbury it was a fateful day for England, a sad destruction of the beloved fatherland, now in the hands of new masters. William of Jumièges, writing only a few years afterwards, heard say that 'in this battle many thousands of the English perished'. William of Poitiers has the English dying by the thousand in the feigned retreats and other incidents of the battle, but never offers a final tally. Most chroniclers are clear, however, that it was a mortal blow to England's ruling class. Poitiers refers to 'the flower of the nobility and youth', Florence of Worcester to 'nearly all the nobility of England' lying dead on the field. The *Anglo-Saxon Chronicle* tersely refers to the 'many good men' that fell with Harold. It was, above all, the death of the king and his brothers that made Hastings one of the most decisive battles in the history of the world. England was under new management. However, some nobles did survive the battle. For example, the thegns Ansgar of Middlesex and Aelfric of Huntingdon lived to fight another day. Harold's faithful housecarl, Scalpi, survived. Yet another survivor was Eadric, a powerful lord in East Anglia who was exiled for his support to Harold in 1066. Eleven out of about twenty known Englishmen were killed in the battle, implying a casualty rate of about fifty per cent. However some of these names are self-selecting; their names were recorded specifically because they were dead, and disputes had arisen over the inheritance of their lands.

Of the thirty-five Normans known to have been present, only

A hero's funeral procession. The Viking Society

five were killed in the battle or died of wounds afterwards, but these were all men of high status. Casualties among the ordinary foot soldiers may have been proportionately higher (they usually were in medieval battles. At Lewes in 1264, at least 2,000 ordinary soldiers were killed, but only three or four men of name). Orderic has 15,000 casualties out of 60,000 combatants; that is, a casualty rate of twenty-five per cent: the numbers are wildly exaggerated, but the ratio is plausible. Perhaps, then, as many as 2,000 Normans and twice that many English were killed or wounded at Hastings. A fifty per cent casualty rate for the English would not, in the circumstances, be surprising. The total number of English dead or disabled in the year 1066 may have approached 10,000, a crippling blow to the warrior caste which goes some way to explain the limpness of England's defence after Hastings. At the best of times, the country was able to sustain about 14,000 men in arms. The events of 1066 destroyed England's ability to defend itself.

Verdict on the battle

Many contemporaries held a low opinion of the fighting qualities of the English. They were undisciplined, and drank too much. William of Malmesbury considered that it was bravado and fury that drove Harold's soldiers at Hastings, rather than military skill. In his view, Harold made a big mistake in taking on William before he was ready:

> 'In this single conflict they doomed themselves and their homeland to slavery, for they allowed William to win an easy victory'.

Though not sharing Malmesbury's opinion that victory had been easy, the Norman sources tend to be even more dismissive of the English. In the speech William of Poitiers puts into the duke's mouth at Hastings, they had never distinguished themselves by deeds of arms. They were inexperienced in war, and so could be overcome by the courage and skill of a few. The *Carmen*, too, likened the English army to so many sheep, or foxes, frightened by thunder. The English victory at Stamford Bridge came as a surprise. The conflicts everyone remembered were the battles against the Danes, earlier in the century, where, for the most part, the English had performed poorly. The Norman writers evidently knew little either about Harold's successful campaigns against the Welsh, nor his fellow earl Siward's against the Scots.

149

The rapid march to York, and their tenacity at Stamford Bridge and Hastings, prove that the English soldiers of 1066 were in fact hardy, brave and, in the right circumstances, formidable. The housecarls, at least, also showed extraordinary discipline and, long afterwards, Snorri Sturlusson considered an English housecarl was worth two of the bravest Vikings. A more telling criticism of the English way of making war is that they seemed hidebound by tradition and slow to adapt to changing circumstances. Though, like the Normans, the English elite went everywhere on horseback, they never seem to have developed cavalry tactics, nor did they employ archers to any great effect (though there must have been plenty of skilled bowmen around). They were one of the last homogenous armies of the western world. In consequence, they stood helpless as the storm of arrows rained down on them, and lacked the mobility to take proper advantage of such opportunities as presented themselves. English tactics, as far as one can see, were resolutely insular and conservative, based on a warrior ethic that had not changed much since the siege of Troy.

The Normans, by contrast, had institutionalised cavalry warfare. It seems that the Norman soldiers were trained to fight in combat units (*conroi*) of five to ten mounted knights or twenty-thirty infantrymen. William's army seems to have disembarked from the ships and formed up to march with great speed and efficiency. They manoeuvred from column to line in the face of the enemy in less than an hour. The successful use of feigned retreat implies an ability to wheel and turn, and then turn again in formation. The archers, too, performed impressively, especially towards the end of the battle when they seem to have suddenly learned how to drop arrows within a narrow zone. Perhaps, like the feigned retreat, Norman archery skills had been learned from contact with the Mediterranean and Byzantine world. Norman cosmopolitanism certainly paid off in 1066.

The Normans were more open to military ideas than the English. They also had more cohesion as a warrior class. Their military environment was highly competitive: the men at Hastings knew one another and had campaigned together. They were used to a highly mobile way of making war, based on ambush and undermining the enemy's capacity by ravaging his lands. The warrior elite, sons of local lords and counts in their twenties, were effectively professional soldiers. Now they were serving in the adventure of their lives, with fortunes to be made, and with justified confidence in their leaders. It helped, too, that Duke William had a reputation for generosity to those that served him well.

Harold has been much criticised for his impetuousness. No modern general would have rushed into action before he was ready, and fallen into the trap the Normans had prepared for him. Harold, according to the tactics of his own age as well as ours, should have put pressure on William by scorched earth tactics, burning ricks and food stores, and, if possible, bringing up the fleet to prevent his escape. And he should have waited until the northern earls had arrived, when Harold would have enough men to take William on in a place of his choosing and beat him. If the chronicles written more than fifty years afterwards can be believed, Harold's captains did indeed make these very points. His brother Gyrth begged Harold not to confront William in person since, as one who had sworn oaths to the duke and accepted knighthood at his hands, he would be at a moral disadvantage. Gyrth could lead the army, and, if he fell, Harold could avenge him. And while Gyrth fought William, Harold should empty the villages, block the roads, burn the stores and lay waste the countryside.

Why did Harold ignore this sensible advice, if such it was? To begin with, he may have lacked the necessary ruthlessness. It was the duty of a king to protect his subjects. In the case of the coastal towns and villages of Sussex, Harold had a double obligation as the local lord. The Godwins had lived in Sussex for three generations, and these were people he knew personally. Another consideration was that winter was approaching, and Harold could not maintain a large force in the field for long without some means of providing for them. The nation had been stood to arms since May, and the system was already strained to the limit. Even the most patriotic had duties to hearth and home, making preparations for the long winter ahead. As for the fleet, the normal season for laying up ships was long past, and Channel gales made sailing difficult and unpredictable. One way or another, time was probably not on Harold's side. In his week in London, he had to come up with a plan and stick to it.

There may be a further reason behind Harold's decision that is only hinted at in the sources. It was probably while in London when he first heard that the Normans were flying the papal banner and William was wearing around his neck the holy relics on which Harold had forsworn himself. Harold would know now that the church had deserted him and found him guilty without hearing a word in his defence. Robert Wace goes further and claims that Harold and his followers had been excommunicated. To an eleventh century sensibility, such news would come as a heavy blow to morale, and it provoked Harold's response: 'let God decide between William and me'. Harold would leave the outcome to the judgement of God, and Hastings would become a trial by battle. This might also go some way to explain why he remained on the field to the bitter end.

Ian Walker, Harold's modern biographer, suggests that he may also have made haste in order to prevent William from breaking out from his beach head at Hastings and running amok in the English countryside, where, with his cavalry and mobile tactics, he would be hard to pin down. The Normans could live off the land, plundering as they went, and throwing up castles to preserve their communications and provide fortified refuges. This is, indeed, more or less what William did after Hastings. Therefore the correct strategy for Harold was to seek to contain William while building his own forces and cutting off Norman supplies.

Wargaming has tended to support the rightness of Harold's decision to stand firm. Christopher Gravett (1992) found that things went well for the English until he was tempted to charge downhill in pursuit: 'My opponent promptly, and rightly, punished such rashness with a brisk counter-attack which proved to be the turning point of the battle - just as in 1066.' Terry Gore (2001) also found that it was best to let the Norman knights batter themselves vainly against the shield-wall. Wargames suggest that the battle might have gone the other way if Harold had had more archers, and reserves to fill the gaps in his ranks. Players soon discover that while William can gallop all over the field, playing Harold is pretty boring, since he has to stay in the same place, crushed inside a crowd of axe-wielding bodyguards.

In the end, Harold probably fought at Hastings because he thought he would win. Although we do not know his battle plan, it seems that his mind was on attack, not defence. He may even have intended to nullify William's advantage in cavalry and archers by the novel tactic of a night attack. He probably did not intend to fight on 14 October, but several days later, and with a superior army. Caldbec Hill was his mustering point, as at Tadcaster before Stamford Bridge, not his chosen battlefield. If so, he was rumbled too soon by William's scouts or spies. The ridge at Senlac therefore became a fall-back position since Harold had been forced back onto the defensive before his plans were ready. William had a better, more modern army, and a bit more luck. But, even so, the Battle of Hastings was a close-run thing.

William: Hastings to London

After 15 October, William returned to his camp at Hastings. He needed to treat the wounded, and rest and provision his tired army. There for five days he waited in vain to receive the submission of the English. On 20 October, leaving an unnamed 'brave commander' at Hastings, William marched out of camp towards Dover. Raiding parties moved ahead, foraging, burning villages and killing anyone who resisted. Manorial records in the *Domesday Book* show that much of the countryside in the path of his march was still 'waste' twenty years afterwards. Romney was punished with fire and sword for its treatment of the stranded French crews before Hastings. Dover surrendered without resistance, and William built his next castle within the old Iron Age fortress above the cliffs on the site of the later Dover castle. Here some of his men contracted dysentery from 'foul water and bad food'. After eight more days, the Normans moved on to Canterbury, which also surrendered. In London there was panic. By now, Edwin and Morcar had arrived in the capital, presumably with reinforcements, and the young Edgar Atheling was recognised (but not crowned) as king. A detachment of Norman cavalry advanced to the Thames at Southwark and skirmished with the English on London Bridge. Realising the Londoners were still capable of defending the Thames bridges, William decided instead to isolate the capital by a march of pillage through the Home Counties. His now reinforced army moved westwards, laying waste the lands of Surrey and Hampshire, and seizing the royal treasure at Winchester, the ancient capital of the Saxon kings.

By now, Saxon resistance was crumbling. At Wallingford, in mid-November, Archbishop Stigand went over to William as he prepared to cross the Thames. Further on, at Berkhamsted in Hertfordshire, William was met by Edgar, Ealdred, the Archbishop of York and other magnates who submitted to him

The Coronation of William the Conqueror at Westminster Abbey on Christmas Day 1066. Outside his men were torching nearby buildings.

154

The Great Seal of William the Conqueror.

'out of necessity'. This effectively was the end. The English, lacking an experienced leader, were unable or unwilling to face William's dreaded cavalry in the field. According to the 'E' Chronicle, 'men made him tribute, and gave him hostages, and then redeemed their lands from him'. Edwin and Morcar saw the writing on the wall, and either surrendered themselves at this point or fled northwards. Both were soon in William's hands as hostages. William entered London and was crowned King of England at Westminster on Christmas Day, 1066. William the Bastard had become William the Conqueror. The hands that lowered the crown, Bishop Ealdred's, were the same as those that had crowned King Harold, just under a year ago. At the shout of acclamation, some of William's soldiers, mistaking it for a riot, set neighbouring houses on fire. Fittingly, smoke began to fill the abbey as the ceremony was hastily concluded.

Ringed: The traditional site of King Harold's tomb is marked by a slab and an upright stone in what used to be the choir of Waltham Abbey.

Hastings, as it turned out, was a rare example of a truly decisive battle. Before it, England had stood to arms for nearly six months, beaten one of the largest Viking armies ever to invade our shores, and confronted the Normans with a sizeable force only three weeks later. Yet after Hastings, resistance withered on the vine. The immediate reason was the irreplaceable loss of a charismatic leader, King Harold.

The only statue of King Harold? A Victorian monument by the west porch of Waltham Abbey commemorates a clean shaven Harold as founder of the abbey.

The only person who might have fitted his shoes, Harold's brother Gyrth, had also perished at Hastings. Edgar Atheling was too young and inexperienced to be more than a nominal figurehead, and the same was true of the northern earls or Harold's male children. There was evidently dissension in London - some were for fighting on, others for submitting to fate. Continuing to resist William would ensure the confiscation of men's lands. Some did, and were exiled. But many must have hoped that King William would at least be no worse than King Canute. Life would, with luck, get back to normal.

The other reason was that England had experienced the eleventh century equivalent of total war for nearly a year. Large areas of the country had been ravaged. Back in November 1065, the northern rebels had laid waste to the country around Northampton, slaying men and burning houses and grainstores, and carrying off all the livestock they could find. They also, according to the 'D' Chronicle, took many hundreds of captives back north 'so that that shire and other neighbouring shires were for many years the poorer'. The south and east coast had suffered raids by Tostig, and, later, by Harald Hardrada. Duke William's march of destruction had taken in much of Sussex and Kent, followed by a swathe of burning and looting through Harold's earldom of Wessex. Countless English men and women had lost their lands and were made homeless that winter. Many of their natural leaders were dead or on the run. Unfortunately for the English, the Normans were not like Canute's Danes. They were not interested in becoming naturalised Englishmen, but rather their masters. King William's men helped themselves to England's wealth. If, after Hastings, the English were in a state of shock, and attributed Harold's fall to God's judgement on their sins, who can blame them? As Ian Walker (1997) comments, perhaps only those who survived the German occupation of the Channel Islands in the Second World War can understand what it must have been like to be an English man or woman in the winter of 1066.

Chapter 11

THE BATTLEFIELDS

Names of battlefields

The Battle of Hastings is unusual in that it commemorates a town far from the battlefield. A more accurate name would be the Battle of Battle! Even in 1066, there were settlements nearer than Hastings that could have lent their names to the battlefield, like Sedlescombe or Harold's own manor at Crowhurst. To the Anglo-Saxon chronicler, it was the battle '*at the hoary apple tree*', the landmark tree where Harold had mustered his army. Another name that was in use within a generation of the battle is Senlac. This is the Norman-French form of the Old English, *Sandlacu*, and means 'sandy water'. It was probably the name of the stream crossing the battlefield, but has gained an extra frisson because in French it means 'lake of blood'. The name survived as Sandlake, a former tithing (a small district for church-rents) of the town of Battle. Some historians have preferred Senlac to Hastings, on grounds of proximity. However, the *Domesday Book* in several places refers unambiguously to '*bellum Haestingas*', that is, the battle at, or of, Hastings. That being so, it was referred to as the Battle of Hastings in the Conqueror's own lifetime. The town was William's base before the battle, and the nearest settlement of any size. And our battles usually are named after nearby towns or settlements, rather than natural features like streams (Sedgemoor and Roundway Down are two obvious exceptions).

For Stamford Bridge, there is no such ambiguity. The battle is referred to by that name from the start, notably in the *Anglo-Saxon Chronicle* [as *Stanfordbrycg*]. Geoffrey Gaimer refers to it as '*Punt de la Bataille*' or 'bridge of battle'. As for Fulford, the Chronicle refers only to a battle 'outside York', while Florence of Worcester mentions 'a battle...on the northern bank of the river Ouse near York'. It may therefore have been known as the Battle of York. The first specific mention of a battle at Fulford [*Fuleford*] is by Simeon of Durham in the twelfth century. In more recent times it has sometimes become the Battle of Gate Fulford, which was the name of the parish before it was joined with the neighbouring Water Fulford in the nineteenth century. The Battle of York might seem a good enough name, since it was fought in defence of that city and within sight of its walls. Unfortunately York has seen a lot of battles, not least the rising of 1065, and another one five years later which left the town in ruins.

The Battlefield of Fulford

Fulford is an ancient settlement listed in the *Domesday Book* (as *Foleford*), and so almost certainly present in 1066. It probably lay along the Roman road to York, on the rising land above the river marshes, as the older houses of the village do today. The battle was fought on marshland between the River Ouse and the village around the watercourse of the Germany Beck, two kilometres south of the city walls of York at Grid Reference SE 608488. The flank of both armies rested on the river, a broad sluggish watercourse about thirty metres wide which flows between steep banks. The lines probably extended eastwards onto higher, drier ground presently occupied by school playing fields and a golf course. Given its proximity to the City of York, Fulford is a surprisingly serene and well-preserved battlefield. It lies on the kind of wet floodland known in this area as Ings. Despite past attempts to drain it, this area is still natural marshland, well-known locally for its pink drifts of bistort and other wild flowers. An ancient track known as the Minster Way runs along the willow-lined river bank past the battlefield and on under the A64 bypass road towards the ruined Bishop's palace at Bishopthorpe.

In 1066, the river floodland seems to have been open, and was perhaps, as today, a village common grazed by ponies, cattle and sheep. Several hedges now cross the marshes at right angles to the river, some of them lining field drains. The most substantial water course, the Germany Beck, was long ago straightened and

A view of Fulford battlefield, long preserved as a village green, and more recently, as Site of Special Scientific Interest.

deepened as a drain, but still marks the area where the two armies clashed. In 1066 its surroundings were probably wetter, perhaps a tidal swamp. Curiously, the ground is driest near the river and wettest, often with standing water, near the village where Morcar's division lay. The terrain is flat, though rising to the south where Harald Hardrada's men first sighted the walls of York and the Saxons advancing towards them.

The battlefield is still wild enough today to have been notified by English Nature, in 1991, as Fulford Ings Site of Special Scientific Interest (SSSI). In its words, the site is an 'important example of flood plain mire located on low lying land between the River Ouse and Fulford village'. We can be fairly confident that the wild flowers we see there today - among them great burnet,

The River Wharfe at Tadcaster. In 1066, a Saxon church stood on the same site as the present church within Roman walls.

pepper saxifrage, meadowsweet, great willowherb and bulrush - were present in 1066. Such things do not change much over time. The battle was fought in early September at the start of a spell of

The motte and bailey of a twelfth century Norman castle stands nearby.

MOTTE

warm weather. By then, the marsh hay had been cut and was perhaps drying in stacks, perfuming the air. The great crack willows on the banks were just starting to yellow, and swallows were gathering for their great winter journey. The thousands of mailed warriors would have trodden the ground into a quagmire.

Fulford field can be reached easily along the Minster Way, either from the City of York or from Fulford village along the track signposted Landing Lane, just north of the York bypass at SE 612487. The well signposted path from the City begins at the steps by Skeldergate Bridge, with fine views of Clifford's Tower and York Castle, before taking the walker past suburban houses, a wireless mast and a pumping station to the beautiful church tower of St Oswalds. Once there, after the bustle and traffic noise, the open fields of Fulford Ings come as a welcome surprise. A tour of the battlefield can be made part of a longer walk to Bishopthorpe via the old railway viaduct, now used as a footbridge, returning by the historic Ebor Way, a track running along the west bank of the river. The walk can end or start at the conveniently situated Yorvik Museum at Coppergate in the City centre, which provides a wonderfully vivid evocation of life in the City during the Viking age.

In 2003, the integrity of the battlefield was threatened by a proposed access road to run from the flood-prone A19 at Fulford across what are still open fields to join an already congested route to the city. It will run across the marshlands where, in the local Battlefields Group's interpretation of the battle, Morcar's brave Northumbrians were encircled and massacred by the Vikings. The Group are pledged to oppose the development. On this interpretation, the battlefield of Fulford is larger than that at Hastings or Stamford Bridge and arguably is closer to the landscape of 1066 than either. Unfortunately, Fulford is the neglected Cinderella of the three great battles of 1066, and, unlike the other two, has not been registered as a historic battlefield by English Heritage.

Parts of the battlefield has been examined with metal detectors by the Fulford Battle Group, but whether the ambiguous-looking bits of rusted metal found there have any connection with the battle is, as yet, uncertain. Some excavations showed signs of earth tipping over the years, perhaps in attempts to improve the pasture and shore up the river bank.

The Battlefield of Stamford Bridge

The village of Stamford Bridge almost certainly existed in 1066. The site lies on the junction of four Roman roads, and, moreover, sits by the navigable River Derwent. Stamford Bridge was also a boundary town, where the North Riding and the East Riding of Yorkshire meet. The village lies amid good farmland, and it would not be surprising if the present large corn mill had a Saxon predecessor: water mill technology, using mill leats to harness the power of fast-flowing rivers like the Derwent, was well-developed in the Saxon age. We should therefore imagine the battlefield as containing a significant settlement, as well as a river bridge, probably in the vicinity of the present day Village Square. The Vikings had no doubt requisitioned the mill and its storage barns as a supply depot for grain and barrels of preserved meat looted from nearby Godwin lands. Stamford Bridge lay in a part of England long under Dane law, and some of the nearby placements, like Skirpenbeck, Bugthorpe, Fangfoss and Aldby, suggest that some of the local population was of Danish ancestry.

Nothing of the '*Stanfordbrycg*' of 1066 survives, at least, not above ground. The present bridge, a handsome single-arched structure built in the 1730s, lies some distance downstream of the earlier bridge, beyond the weir and a cut made to power a factory (presently the McKechnie plastics factory). The probable site of the bridge of 1066 was discovered by Colonel Alfred Burne, and is described in detail in his *More Battlefields of England* (1952). Burne noticed that the four ancient roads that meet at Stamford Bridge would naturally intersect at a point some 370 metres

Where the battlefield used to be...

upstream of the present bridge. Sure enough, when he walked the ground he discovered traces of ancient trackways along the expected lines of the minor road running south from Primrose Hill, of the broad verged Roman road (the A166) running beyond the present sharp bend over the bridge, and of the Minster Way on the far bank. The tracks, there for Burne to find in 1950, were still partially visible twenty years on when Colonel Howard Green investigated the site (Green 1973). The old bridge must have lain just upstream of the weir, and, in Green's view, rocks used to build the weir must once have carried the wooden piers of the Saxon bridge. Unfortunately the site has since become more cluttered by buildings and permanent caravans. Earth movers have been allowed to shovel up the precious trackway evidence to build bays for the mobile homes and platforms for the new houses. A bungalow sits in its earth-moulded garden astride the old line of the main road, and private gardens obscure what evidence may survive on the east bank. However, a right of way running between garden fences from the A166 to join Moor Road on the Minster Way must mark the line of one of the 'lost roads' (it is marked on the 1:50,000 map at SE 716556). The Vikings probably used this track to form up on the 'Battle Flats' on the higher ground east of the river.

The recently renovated Stamford Bridge battle monument by the roadside (A166) at the entrance to the Corn Mill.

The Battle Flats themselves give little away apart from the name. The Flats nearest to the river has been built over, with streets, including the inevitable 'Viking Way' and 'Battleflats

A plaque set into the courtyard wall is easier to read than the tarnished brass plates on the battle stone.

THE BATTLE OF STAMFORD BRIDGE

KING HAROLD OF ENGLAND DEFEATED HIS BROTHER TOSTIG AND KING HARDRAADA OF NORWAY HERE ON 25 SEPTEMBER 1066

Way', running between modest brick houses and bungalows. Beyond that, the old Minster Way, now a minor road, winds between hedges past the huge arable fields characteristic of this part of Yorkshire. The English Heritage registered battlefield encloses about 400 acres of featureless ploughland just east of the village. There, according to tradition, the Vikings formed up after crossing the river. Perhaps, then, this was the site of the piles of whitened bones noted by Orderic Vitalis. However a stronger position would have been closer to the river, since it would force King Harold's men to attack uphill from the boggy ground by the river - in a reversal of the battle of Hastings. Unfortunately this part of the battlefield is covered by houses, gardens and streets. However a good view of the still unobscured river terrace can be had from the footpath near the old railway viaduct at SE 711555.

There are several reminders of the battle in the village, all close together near the area known as The Square. On a roadside bank outside the entrance to the restored corn mill (SE 174556) stands the memorial stone, a rough-hewn boulder with inset brass plaques, stating in English and Norwegian, that 'The Battle of Stamford Bridge was fought in this neighbourhood on September 25th 1066'. Recently a brick courtyard has been built around the stone, and a new plaque built into its wall. Since flagstones now conceal the lower half of the monument, a second stone now perches on top of it. Wooden benches line the sides of the courtyard, and beyond it lies a public garden, with picnic tables and roving gangs of geese and ducks.

The restored Corn Mill at Stamford Bridge, close to the site of the old bridge.

The Cut near the modern bridge was made to power a local factory, now a plastics works. The river works, including the Cut and the weir, made it necessary to build the eighteenth century bridge further downstream, abandoning the ancient crossroads and causing a kink in the main road through the village.

A hundred yards away, by the turning of 'Viking Way' lies another pleasant green with trees, more picnic tables and a free car park. Here the river runs fast, deep and about twenty metres wide through the span of the stone bridge. Nowhere does the river seem fordable, and so taking the Saxon bridge was a vital part of Harold's battle plan. Perhaps the legend of the solo Viking, celebrated on the sign of the nearby pub, The Swordsman (see p.33), enshrines a memory of the stiff resistance made by Viking cover force while Harald Hardrada and Tostig prepared to offer battle on the far bank. This is a good place to begin to explore the battlefield on foot. Inset into the brick wall of a public convenience is another reminder of the battle: a map of the village superimposed on an imaginary view of the battle with crude troll-like figures. The sign also displays the village arms: a Viking longship above the Yorkshire white rose and two crossed axes.

From the car park, the visitor can use the plentiful public footpaths to walk the river bank in both directions, and then to follow the old Minster Way up onto the Battle Flats, returning for refreshments at the corn mill, now a bar and carvery restaurant, or The Swordsman Inn. Finally, a Harold's eye view of the field can be had from Gate Helmsley, which overlooks the field from the west. This is where the Vikings first spotted the Saxon force, their mail and spearpoints 'glittering like ice'. The A166 from Gate Helmsley to Stamford Bridge follows the exact line of the old Roman road taken by the armies of 1066.

Finds from the battlefield are few and undocumented. From time to time the ploughed fields on the Battle Flats have yielded small horseshoes, which may or may not have any link with the battle. Real archaeological evidence would help to pinpoint the exact site of Harald Hardrada's last stand, which at the present time is conjectural. In fact, this decisive but neglected battle cries out for more research, better interpretation - and protection against the new housing estates that threaten to engulf it.

The Battlefield of Hastings

The site of the most famous battle in history is owned by English Heritage, and is open to the public during daylight hours. A full tour of the sites associated with the battle will take a full day, and should include a visit to Pevensey Castle, the site of the Norman landing, and to the clifftop castle at Hastings, where the motte built by William's engineers still stands and where the '1066 Story' is told 'through a fascinating multi-media experience'. If permission can be obtained, it is also worth inspecting the probable site of the Malfosse and the site of the 'hoar apple tree', close to the windmill on Caldbec Hill. A tour of the actual battlefield takes two to three hours, allowing time to wander over the ruins of William's abbey and visit English Heritage's battle museum. Harold's approach march through the woods follows roughly the line of the present A2100 north of Battle; Crowhurst and Battle Woods contain evidence of ancient sunken tracks that may well have been in use in 1066. William's initial position on Telham Hill can be reached by road. The actual hilltop is now within a nature reserve of the Sussex Wildlife Trust. The remains of the medieval manor house at nearby Crowhurst - probably on the site of Harold's manor - can be seen. The churchyard has a yew tree said to be over a thousand years old. If so, it may be the sole living witness of the Norman atrocities which brought Harold hurrying from London before his forces were fully gathered.

The battlefield itself is thoroughly 'interpreted'. The visitor is offered an instrument resembling a mobile phone that produces a taped commentary at a touch of a button, corresponding with numbered posts on the battlefield. There are eight 'table models' that illustrate particular stages of the battle from particular viewpoints, and a written tour guide of the Abbey and the battlefield is available at the shop in the Abbey gatehouse. The well signposted circular path over that part of the battlefield in English Heritage ownership is just over a mile, and, with pauses for inward contemplation of the scene, takes about an hour and a half. However, it is worth extending the tour using permissive paths on private land to the west of the Abbey for a view of the Norman left wing and the gorse-crowned hillock plausibly identified with the hillock shown on the Bayeux Tapestry.

The slope up which the Normans advanced to engage the Saxons is still natural grassland, and still wet in places. The field as a whole is attractive parkland with mature trees - probably more than were present in 1066, but which may otherwise be little changed. However the marsh and ditches which formed a severe obstacle for the Norman horse has been much reduced by the formation of a series of ponds along the line of the brook. The top of the ridge where the Saxon shield-wall stood was partly levelled shortly after the battle when building work began on the Abbey. However one can still gain a vivid Saxon's - eye view of the field from the fine terrace that runs across Harold's position. The easternmost segment of the battlefield has been effectively lost: William's right wing probably advanced close to the present A2100 (which cuts into the ridge) on now built-up land between Battle railway station and the twelfth century church of St Mary the Virgin (which contains a stained glass window commemorating 'the Battle of Senlac'). The easternmost point of the ridge is marked by the former Battle primary school. But the square kilometre or so of open land registered by English Heritage as the Battlefield is well preserved by the standards of most medieval battlefields. There is surprisingly little to say about its archaeology. The battlefield has never been excavated scientifically, and finds from the field are few and unrevealing. Probably the field had been thoroughly looted and cleared within days of the battle. Possibly also the acidic soils of the Hastings beds would make short work of any iron swords or chain mail buried in the soil.

A tour of the battlefield should begin with the visitor centre, currently housed in a prefabricated building discretely camouflaged by trees close to the gatehouse. The exhibition tells the story of 1066 from the different English and Norman viewpoints, making much use of the Bayeux Tapestry. Outside is an audiovisual showing of the battle using the voices of three participants: a Saxon thegn, a Norman knight (who gets the thegn's lands) and King Harold's Danish-law wife, Edith Swanneck. The tour starts close by with the first table model, revealing a fine view of the western part of the field from the English position. The tour continues southwards down the slope, but many will be tempted, as I was, to first walk along the Abbey terrace to take in the views across the battlefield towards the wooded Telham Hill on the horizon. As shown on the map, table model No. 4 rests on a slight rise between the ridge and the largest of the ponds ('New Pond') in an area known as Horselodge Plantation, which English Heritage interpret as the famous hillock. Table model No. 5, down in the valley, may be where Duke William rallied his knights after their first unsuccessful charge. From there the tour continues along the valley before climbing back up the slope to reach the abbey ruins.

Having regained the terrace, take the steps past the gable end of the monk's dormitory, the most substantial part of the Abbey still standing, which take you to the site of the Abbey church and Harold's command post. The position of the High Altar, which probably marks the very place where the King's body was found after the battle, is marked by an inscribed slab (see page 136). A few yards away is another, older monument, with its inscription in Norman French: '*Diex aie*' - 'God aid us', the cry of the Normans on the morning of 14 October 1066. From there, if time permits, it is worth walking up Battle High Street, formed on a natural ridge of ground, to the top of Caldbec Hill, Harold's muster point, reached along Mount Street. From here, the hammer headed contours of Senlac ridge can be appreciated, and the landscape reveals why William was compelled to attack Harold frontally. Steep slopes surround the ridge on all sides except the narrow neck of land along the present High Street. Another good viewpoint is Powdermill Lane (B2095), which runs along the southern boundary of the field. This name, with its echoes of later military technology, commemorates a former gunpowder mill, based on charcoal from local alder trees. According to Daniel Dafoe, Battle produced 'the finest gunpowder in England, and probably the best in Europe'. Unfortunately, a tall hedge obscures the view from the lane, and there are few roadside parking opportunities. Like most compact medieval battlefields, Hastings is best explored on foot.

The Abbey Gatehouse houses a shop and a small museum displaying artifacts from the Abbey. The Abbey and the battlefield are open from 10 to 6 (April-September), 10 to 5 in October and 10 to 4 in winter (November-March), admission £4.50 (children under 15, £2.30, concession £3.40, family ticket £11.30).

Battle Abbey

Gable end of the monk's dormitory, at Battle Abbey. Steps to the left lead up from the terrace to where Harold's standard flew at Hastings.

Should we be thankful for Battle Abbey? Because its construction was supervised by the Conqueror himself, we can be sure that it marks the exact place where Harold's fallen banner and body were found after the battle. The whole abbey is, in effect, a battle monument. On the other hand, its construction has meant that the original contours of the field are lost forever. Harold actually stood not on the flattish ground of the present day abbey ruins but several feet above it! The battlefield was the property of the monks throughout the Middle Ages, who probably used it to graze flocks and provide fish on Fridays from the 'stew ponds' built by damming the Ashen Brook (the largest of the ponds, the New Pond, was constructed much later, in 1815). The Abbey, founded in 1070, less than four years after the battle, was unsentimentally demolished by Sir Anthony Brown in the 1540s, and its stone and roofing lead recycled around the town. Fortunately the medieval gatehouse survives, and forms as grand an entrance to a battlefield as any visitor could wish.

The best-known story is that Duke William vowed on the morning of the battle to found a great abbey on the lonely hilltop if God granted him victory. The alternative, which is documented rather than simply told as a story, is that the abbey was imposed on him by the Pope as an atonement for the blood spilt during the Norman Conquest. Whatever the truth of the matter, monks from the Benedictine abbey of Marmoutier on the Loire were invited to found a great abbey on the battlefield, starting with the church. Like William's castles, this was to be a French creation, though it may be that English masons lacked experience of stonework on this scale. Like Westminster Abbey, Battle Abbey was to be in the Norman style of the Romanesque, based on the still-standing abbey at Jumièges. Grand religious foundations like this took a long time to build. Even with royal revenues being poured into their construction, Westminster Abbey took sixteen years, and Battle Abbey twenty-four. For a quarter century after the Battle of Hastings, the site must have swarmed with construction workers, while Senlac ridge was crossed again and again by carters bringing in loads of Caen limestone from the ships at Hastings.

The part of William the Conqueror that thought about the hereafter was much concerned with the Abbey. There was a row when he heard that, having surveyed the ground, the monks had found it unsuitable and disobeyed him by starting work at a better site further west. They were made to begin again on the stoneless, waterless ridge, surrounded by woods and marshes, indicating that the king attached great importance to the exact positioning of the church. Its High Altar was to be situated on the very spot where Harold had fallen, whose position, according to the *Battle Abbey Chronicle,* had been carefully marked. There was an obvious parallel here with ancient Rome, where Constantine's basilicas were raised over the exact site of St Peter's martyrdom and what purported to be Christ's nativity. However, unlike St Peter, Harold's body would not rest at Battle - as an oathbreaker, he had no place in William's foundation. The still-uncompleted Abbey was in William's thoughts as he lay gasping on his deathbed at St Gervais near Rouen in 1087. He left the monks a collection of precious relics, a portable altar and, as a symbolic gift, his royal cloak. Battle Abbey had been dedicated to St Martin of Tours, who had become a Christian after giving up his cloak to a blind beggar.

The Abbey was eventually consecrated in 1094, in the presence of the Conqueror's son, King William Rufus, and the Archbishop of Canterbury, Anselm. It was the first major Norman church to be completed. Unfortunately, virtually nothing of the original foundation survives today. The only scrap of original Norman stonework is in a wall incorporating part of the south aisle of the abbey church. The gatehouse and other buildings there today are fourteenth century additions, made at a time when war with

Lost contours. Ground levelled at the western side of Hastings battlefield to form a school playing field.

France necessitated high walls for wealthy properties near the Channel coast.

The main surviving building is the Abbot's House, which was taken over by Sir Anthony Brown, a courtier and crony of Henry VIII, in 1540, whose painted tomb lies in the church of St Mary close by. The house later passed to the Webster family. A fire in 1931 destroyed much of the interior, but, duly restored, it now forms part of the private Battle Abbey School. In 1976, the Gatehouse and abbey ruins, along with part of the battlefield, were purchased by the government, whose agency, English Heritage, now administers the site.

The Vikings

CELTIC, NORMAN, SAXON & VIKING RE-ENACTMENT

Founded in 1971, The Vikings are the oldest and largest Dark Age re-enactment society in the UK, and probably the world. With over 700 members throughout Britain, and others in Europe and the US, The Vikings are the premier society presenting re-enactments of the Viking Age. While the Society concentrates mainly on the tenth century, some events are set in the wider period from 790 to 1066, with the appropriate modifications to dress and equipment used. Our aim is to provide an accurate and educational portrayal of the Viking period, with an equal emphasis on the daily life of the period, and on the more warlike aspects of life in what was a formative period in European history.

Our events are renowned for the high standard of presentation, historical accuracy and attention to detail, and for the scale and impact of our combat displays, as well as for our extensive static displays which present a cross-section of life in the tenth century. Whether you are interested in booking The Vikings for your event, coming to watch our displays, joining the ranks of our membership, or studying the Viking Age in either an educational or personal setting, we hope The Vikings has something to offer.

To find out more or to book an event, please visit The Vikings Website at:

www.vikingsonline.org.uk
or email
events@vikingsonline.org.uk

Or contact the Society's Special Events Coordinator:
Roger Barry
19 Boundary Road
Laverstock
Salisbury
SP1 1RN

Telephone: 01722 504775

REFERENCES AND FURTHER READING

Bachrach, Bernard (1971) *The Feigned Retreat at Hastings*. *Medieval Studies*, 344-47, reprinted in Morillo (1996), pp190-93.

Barlow, Frank, (1970) *Edward the Confessor*. Methuen, London. The standard biography.

Barlow, Frank, (2002) *The Godwins*. The rise and fall of a noble dynasty. Longman, Edinburgh and London. Full of insights by the leading scholar of eleventh century England.

Brooks, F.W. (1956) *The Battle of Stamford Bridge*. East Yorks Local History Society.

Burne, Alfred H., (1950) *The Battle of Hastings*. In: The Battlefields of England. Methuen, London, pp 19-45.

Chevallier, C.T., (1963) *Where was Malfosse? Sussex Archaeological Collections*, 101.

Crouch, David, (2002) *The Normans. A History of a Dynasty*. Hambledon & London, London. Immensely readable, gives the Norman perspective, including a masterly summary of how William won the war of propaganda.

Douglas, David C., (1964) *William the Conqueror. The Norman impact upon England*. Methuen, London. Especially Chapter 8, 'The Conquest of England, pp181-210.

Douglas, D.C. & Greenaway, G.W. (2nd edn 1981) *English Historical Documents*, Vol 2, 1042-1189. Oxford University Press. Includes translations of William of Poitiers, William of Jumièges, 'Florence' of Worcester, *Anglo-Saxon Chronicle* and the Bayeux Tapestry, and other documents relating to the battle, as well as a summary of the events of 1066.

Fletcher, Richard, (2002) *Bloodfeud. Murder and revenge in Anglo-Saxon England*. Allen Lane, London. Insightful account of the dark side of the eleventh century.

Freeman, E.A., (3rd edn, 1877) *The History of the Norman Conquest of England, its Causes and Results*. 3 volumes, Oxford.

Fry, Plantagenet Somerset, (1990) *The Battle of Hastings 1066 and the story of Battle Abbey*. English Heritage.

Fuller, J.F.C., (1954) *The Battle of Hastings, 1066. A Military History of the Western World,* Minerva Press, pp374-82. Reprinted in Morillo (1996), pp166-71.

Garmonsway, G.N., (1954) *The Anglo-Saxon Chronicle*. Everyman's Library.

Gillmor, C.M. (1996) *Naval logistics of the cross-channel operation, 1066.* In: Morillo (1996), pp114-28.

Glover, Richard, (1952) *English warfare in 1066.* English Historical *Review,* 67, 1-18, reprinted in Morillo (1996a), pp174-88.

Gore, Terry L. (2001) *The Anglo-Saxon army of Harold Godwinson 1066 AD.* www.saga-publishing.com.

Gravett, Christopher (1992) *Hastings 1066. The fall of Saxon England.* Campaign Series. Osprey Publishing, London. Well-illustrated summary.

Higham, N.J., (1997) *The Death of Anglo-Saxon England.* Sutton Publishing, Stroud. Especially good on the Viking invasion of 1066, pp182-97.

Howarth, David, (1978) *1066: The Year of the Conquest.* Penguin Books, London. Readable, fast-moving account for the general reader.

John, Eric, (1982) *The End of Anglo-Saxon England.* In: *The Anglo-Saxons,* ed. James Campbell. Phaidon Press. pp214-239.

Kerner, Sten (1964) *The Battle of Hastings: England and Europe 1035-1066.* Gleerup, Lund.

Lawson, M.K., (2002) *The Battle of Hastings 1066.* Tempus Publishing, Stroud. Detailed look at the sources and the battlefield.

Magnusson, Magnus & Palsson, Hermann (1966) *King Harald's Saga. Harald Hardradi of Norway, from Snorri Sturluson's Heimskringla.* Penguin Books, London.

Morillo, Stephen, (1996) *The Battle of Hastings. Sources and interpretations.* Boydell & Brewer, Woodbridge, Suffolk. Indispensable guide to the battle, including all the main sources and classic modern accounts.

Morillo, Stephen (1996) *Hastings, an unusual battle.* In: Morillo (1996), pp220-227.

Muntz, Hope (1949) *The Golden Warrior: the Story of Harold and William.* Chatto & Windus, London. The best-ever fictional novel of Harold, solidly based on contemporary sources.

Nicolle, David, (1987) *The Normans.* Osprey Publishing Ltd, London.

Pollington, Stephen, (1996) *The English Warrior from earliest times to 1066.* Anglo-Saxon Books, Norfolk. Useful source on arms and warfare.

Pollock, J. (1996) *Is King Harold buried in Bosham Church?* Penny Royal Publications.

Rathbone, Julian, (1977) *The Last English King.* Little Brown, London. The twentieth century meets the eleventh.

Richards, Julian, (2001) *Blood of the Vikings.* Hodder & Stoughton, London. Chapter 11, 'The Final Stand', pp205-31, has some details of recent excavations at York and Riccall.

Rud, Mogens, (1988) *The Bayeux Tapestry.* SPA Books, Stevenage.

Stafford, Pauline, (1977) *Queen Emma and Queen Edith.* Blackwell, Oxford. A feminist view with new insights into the political role of eleventh century queens.

Stenton, F. (1965) *The Bayeux Tapestry. A comprehensive survey.* Phaidon, London.

Stenton, Frank (3rd ed 1971) *Anglo-Saxon England.* Oxford University Press, especially Chapter 16, 'The Norman Conquest', pp581-596.

Thorpe, Lewis, (1973) *The Bayeux Tapestry and the Norman invasion.* Folio Society, London. Contains a translation of the relevant parts of *Gesta Guillelmi* by William of Poitiers.

Walker, Ian W., (1997) *Harold, the last Anglo-Saxon king.* Sutton & Co, Stroud. Carefully documented biography of King Harold.

Wright, Peter Poyntz, (1996) *Hastings.* Windrush Press, Moreton-in-Marsh. Great Battles series.

Acknowledgements

I should like to thank the following for their help and support:

Ian Muirhead and The Vikings for their generosity in allowing us to use six images taken by Steve Reeve of Ferry View Photography. Chas Jones and the York Battlefield Group for their help over Fulford and permission to include the Group's interpretation of that battle. Steve Berry and Pat Millard for their convivial hospitality while I was exploring '1066 Country'. Mr Phillip Merricks for showing me around Rye and Romney Marsh, and, in the course of an animated conversation about the Normans, well remembered in those parts, for mentioning neighbours of his who are in direct descent from men who came over with the Conqueror. John and Emily Finnie for sustaining me before my journey north in King Harold's footsteps, and William to whom this book is affectionately dedicated. Brigadier Henry Wilson and Barbara Bramall for their encouragement and interest, and Jon Wilkinson for so splendidly turning my rough sketches into art. Jon Cooksey, editor of *Battlefields Review* for suggesting the idea. And to the memory of Hope Muntz, whose novel The *Golden Warrior* nearly forty years ago sparked my interest in the events of the fateful year 1066.

The Author

Peter Marren is a writer and journalist who specialises in nature conservation issues and military history. He is the author of *Grampian Battlefields*, a study of conflict in north-east Scotland, which was runner-up for the Saltire Prize in 1990. An active member of the Battlefields Trust, he has contributed originally researched articles to *Battlefield Review* on Dark Age and medieval battles, including Tewkesbury, Lewes, Evesham and Harlaw. He has visited and walked over most British battlefields. Author of fourteen books of biography, bibliography, history and natural history, he lives in the country in Wiltshire.

INDEX